ALMOST HOMEMADE
CAKE MIX DESSERTS

ALMOST HOMEMADE

CAKE MIX DESSERTS

This cookbook is a collection of our favorite recipes,
which are not necessarily original recipes.

Published by

FRP

P.O. Box 305142
Nashville, Tennessee 37230
1-800-358-0560

Copyright © 2006 by

FRP

Cover Photograph © Jupiter Images

ISBN: 0-87197-522-X

Manufactured in China
First Printing: 2006

Additional cookbooks by **FRP**

My Favorite Recipes: Capture Your Family's Favorite Recipes and Traditions

Quick & Easy Grilling: Over 100 Fast & Furious Timesaving Recipes

The Vintner's Table: Recipes from a Winery Chef

To order these and many other award-winning cookbooks,
visit www.cookbookmarketplace.com or www.frpbooks.com,
or call 1-800-269-6839.

Contents

Better Baking Tips

- Follow the recipe instructions carefully.

- Use proper measuring utensils for liquid and dry ingredients.

- Always use the pan size called for in the recipe.

- The temperature indicated in recipes for most baked goods is suitable for use with metal pans. If you are using glass bakeware, reduce the oven temperature by 25 degrees to prevent overbaking.

- Dark bakeware absorbs more heat and therefore cooks food faster than light bakeware. You may need to adjust the baking time and/or baking temperature to get the end result you want. Dark pans will cause cakes that contain sugar and eggs to burn on the outside before the inside is done. Dark baking sheets can also cause fast-cooking cookies to scorch on the bottom.

- Unless otherwise specified, have ingredients ready at room temperature.

- Don't use a cake mix with pudding inside if you are following a recipe that calls for instant pudding as an ingredient.

- Always preheat your oven at least 12 to 15 minutes before baking a cake.

- Each oven heats differently, so the first time you try a recipe, check the cake 5 minutes before its minimum cooking time ends.

- Place cake pans on the middle oven rack, making sure that they don't touch each other or the sides of the oven. If they are on separate racks, stagger them so air can circulate.

- Always leave 1 to 2 inches between cookies dropped on a cookie sheet to allow them room to spread.

- Place cookie dough on a cool cookie sheet; it will spread on a hot one.

- Do not use butter or margarine to grease cookie sheets, as it will burn easily and cause the bottoms of cookies to become too brown. Use shortening, spreading it evenly over the surface of the cookie sheet.

- Cookie sheets without rims are best for even browning of cookies. Those with high sides deflect the heat and make cookies hard to remove.

Finishing Touches

- To prevent the top layer of a layer cake from slipping as you frost it, insert a wire cake tester or thin skewers through all layers. Remove the tester just before completing the job.

- Make a quick and easy topping for a cake by placing a paper doily on the top and sprinkling it lightly with confectioners' sugar. Carefully lift the doily from the cake.

- Avoid white streaks on the side of your chocolate bundt cake by dusting the greased pan with baking cocoa instead of flour.

- If you do not have a pastry bag, spoon a small amount of frosting into a small plastic bag. Press out as much air as possible and seal. Snip a tiny opening in the corner of the bag, and squeeze the frosting through the opening.

- To keep crumbs out of the frosting when frosting a cake, spread a thin layer of frosting over the top and side of the cake with a metal spatula. Let the frosting set briefly before spreading the remaining frosting over the cake.

- For smooth frosting, dip a long metal spatula into a glass of very hot water. Wipe the spatula dry, and gently smooth the frosting on the cake.

- Make borders for frosted cakes by using chocolate-dipped whole almonds or strawberries, white chocolate or chocolate chips, gumdrops, or jelly beans.

- Use miniature marshmallows as candleholders on birthday cakes to keep the candle wax from dripping onto the frosting.

- Jazz up plain brownies by topping them with chocolate chips, white chocolate chips, peanut butter chips, shredded coconut, or toffee bits while still hot.

- Insert wooden sticks into large sugar cookies before baking to make clever cookie-on-a-stick party favors for children of all ages. Decorate the cookies to suit the occasion.

- Use frosting to pipe names of guests on rectangular cookies for place cards.

Cake Mix Solutions

If an afternoon of baking together sounds wonderful but never seems to happen, maybe you need a shortcut.

If you've ever baked a cake or cookies from scratch, you know it's a long process that includes creaming, separating eggs, and folding. If you include homemade frosting, you could be in the kitchen all day. Maybe that's why all those cookbooks of old favorites stare at you, unopened, from the cookbook shelf. Who has the time?

Cake mixes are one solution. The basic ingredients are pre-measured and mixed, saving you time. And a cake mix is a good start on "almost from scratch" desserts and snacks. If you make a habit of keeping cake mix on hand, you'll always have the beginnings of a quick, satisfying dessert. You can decide to bake at the last minute, without making a special trip to the store. Just flip through this cookbook until you find a recipe that uses the ingredients you have. At that moment, you could be less than an hour away from a dessert, snack, or bake sale item.

Creative cooks use cake mixes as a head start on desserts as diverse as Lemon Biscotti, Cherry Dump Dessert, and Cranberry Cobbler. Maybe you just hope to stir up a snack, and something like Cherry Cobbler Bars sounds good. Perhaps you want a cool dessert for hot weather; chilled Blueberry Trifle might be just right. If you're in need of a bit of something creamy and comforting, maybe Pecan Cream Cheese Bars is the recipe for you.

The recipes in this book are so easy to prepare, you may want to try them all. Whatever recipes you choose, one or more will surely become staples that you'll make over and over and that everyone will remember fondly. And perhaps one of these recipes will become a favorite that's passed from generation to generation. That's how recipes become family treasures.

Let Them
Eat Cakes

Fast Carrot Cake

Cake

1 (2-layer) package white
  cake mix
4 eggs
1 cup water
1/2 (16-ounce) can crushed
  pineapple
1/2 cup flaked coconut

1 cup raisins
1 cup chopped pecans or walnuts
1/2 cup vegetable oil
1 3/4 cups shredded carrots
1 teaspoon cinnamon
1/2 to 1 teaspoon allspice, or to taste
1/2 to 1 teaspoon nutmeg, or to taste

Lemon Cream Cheese Frosting

4 ounces cream cheese, softened
1 1/2 cups confectioners' sugar

1 teaspoon (or more) skim milk
1/2 teaspoon lemon extract

For the cake, combine the cake mix, eggs, water, undrained pineapple, coconut, raisins, pecans, oil, carrots, cinnamon, allspice and nutmeg in a bowl and mix well. Pour into a bundt pan sprayed with nonstick cooking spray. Bake at 350 degrees for 40 to 45 minutes or until the cake tests done. Cool in the pan for several minutes. Invert onto a serving plate.

For the frosting, beat the cream cheese in a bowl. Add the confectioners' sugar, skim milk and flavoring and beat until of spreading consistency. Spread over the cake.

Serves 16 to 20

Butterscotch Cake

2 cups milk
1 (4-ounce) package butterscotch
  cook-and-serve pudding

1 (2-layer) yellow cake mix
1 cup butterscotch chips
1/2 cup chopped pecans or walnuts

Combine the milk and pudding mix in a saucepan over medium heat. Cook until thickened, stirring constantly. Remove from the heat. Combine the pudding mixture and cake mix in a mixing bowl and beat until smooth and creamy. Pour the batter into a greased and floured 9x13-inch baking dish. Sprinkle the butterscotch chips and pecans over the top. Bake at 350 degrees for 35 to 40 minutes or until the cake tests done.

Serves 12 to 18

Chocolate-Cherry Angel Food Cake

1 (16-ounce) package angel food
  cake mix
2 (21-ounce) cans cherry pie filling
16 ounces cream cheese, softened

1 (16-ounce) can ready-to-spread
  French vanilla frosting
Chocolate syrup

Prepare and bake the cake mix using the package directions. Invert onto a funnel to cool completely. Drain the cherries. Combine the cream cheese and frosting in a bowl and mix well. Slice the cake horizontally in half. Place 1 half on a cake plate. Drizzle chocolate syrup over the cake. Spread half the cream cheese mixture over the prepared cake. Arrange half the cherries around the edge of the cake. Top with the remaining cake half and repeat the layers. Drizzle with additional chocolate syrup.

Serves 16

Chocolate Cherry Cake

Cake

1 (2-layer) package devil's food
    cake mix
1/2 cup vegetable oil

2 eggs, beaten
1 tablespoon almond extract
1 (21-ounce) can cherry pie filling

Chocolate Glaze

1 cup sugar
5 tablespoons margarine
1/2 cup milk

1 tablespoon almond extract
1 cup chocolate chips

For the cake, combine the cake mix, oil, eggs and almond extract in a bowl and mix well by hand. Stir in the pie filling. Spoon into a greased and floured 10x15-inch cake roll pan. Bake at 350 degrees for 20 minutes or until the cake tests done.

For the glaze, combine the sugar, margarine, milk and almond extract in a saucepan and mix well. Bring to a boil. Cook for 2 minutes, stirring constantly. Remove from the heat. Add the chocolate chips, stirring until blended. Pour over the warm cake.

Serves 24

Chocolate Buttercream Cake

1 (2-layer) package buttercream
  cake mix
1 (4-ounce) package chocolate
  instant pudding mix
1/2 cup water
1/2 cup vegetable oil
1 cup sour cream
3 eggs

1 teaspoon vanilla extract
1 cup semisweet chocolate chips
6 ounces German's sweet chocolate,
  finely chopped
1/2 cup finely chopped walnuts
  or pecans
Confectioners' sugar

Combine the cake mix, pudding mix, water, oil and sour cream in a bowl and mix well.
Add the eggs 1 at a time, beating well after each addition. Stir in the vanilla. Fold in the
chocolate chips, sweet chocolate and walnuts. Pour into a greased and floured bundt pan.

Bake at 350 degrees for 55 to 60 minutes or until the cake tests done. Cool in the
pan for 10 minutes. Invert onto a serving plate. Place a paper doily on the cake. Sift
confectioners' sugar over the doily. Remove the doily carefully.

Serves 16

Chocolate Chip Pound Cake

1 (2-layer) package devil's food
   cake mix
1 cup water

$1/2$ cup vegetable oil
3 eggs
$1/2$ cup chocolate chips

Combine the cake mix, water, oil and eggs in a mixing bowl and beat at low speed for 4 minutes. Fold in the chocolate chips. Pour into a greased tube pan. Bake at 350 degrees for 40 minutes. Cool in the pan for 20 minutes. Invert onto a wire rack to cool completely.

Serves 12

Chocolate Pick-Me-Up Cake

1 (2-layer) package chocolate cake
   mix with pudding
1 cup sour cream
1 cup water
3 eggs

$1/2$ cup sugar
$1/2$ teaspoon cinnamon
$3/4$ cup semisweet chocolate chips
$3/4$ cup coconut

Combine the cake mix, sour cream, water and eggs in a mixing bowl and beat at low speed until moistened. Beat at high speed for 2 minutes. Pour into a greased and floured 9x13-inch cake pan. Combine the sugar, cinnamon, chocolate chips and coconut in a bowl and mix well. Sprinkle the mixture over the top of the cake. Bake at 350 degrees for 30 to 40 minutes or until the cake tests done.

Serves 12

Chocolate-Orange Bundt Cake with Orange Glaze

Cake

1 (2-layer) package devil's food
  cake mix
1 cup nonfat yogurt
2 tablespoons grated orange zest
1/2 cup orange juice

1 egg
2 egg whites
2 tablespoons vegetable oil
1/2 cup water
1 teaspoon cinnamon

Orange Glaze

1/2 cup confectioners' sugar
1/4 teaspoon vanilla extract
1 teaspoon (or more) orange juice
1/2 cup confectioners' sugar

1 tablespoon baking cocoa
1/4 teaspoon vanilla extract
2 teaspoons (or more) orange juice

For the cake, spray the bundt pan with nonstick cooking spray and dust with baking cocoa. Combine the cake mix, yogurt, orange zest, orange juice, egg, egg whites, oil, water and cinnamon in a mixing bowl and beat for 4 minutes. Spoon into the prepared pan. Bake at 350 degrees for 40 to 50 minutes or until the cake tests done. Cool in the pan for 10 minutes. Invert onto a serving plate.

For the glaze, blend 1/2 cup confectioners' sugar, 1/4 teaspoon vanilla and 1 teaspoon orange juice in a bowl. Drizzle over the cake. Blend 1/2 cup confectioners' sugar, the baking cocoa, 1/4 teaspoon vanilla and 2 teaspoons orange juice in a bowl. Drizzle over the cake.

Serves 12

Chocolate Praline Cake

1 cup packed brown sugar
$1/2$ cup (1 stick) butter
  (no substitute)
$1/4$ cup heavy cream or
  evaporated milk
$3/4$ cup chopped pecans

1 (2-layer) package devil's food
  cake mix
$13/4$ cups whipping cream
$1/4$ cup confectioners' sugar
$1/4$ teaspoon vanilla extract

Combine the brown sugar, butter and heavy cream in a saucepan. Cook over low heat until the butter is melted, stirring constantly. Pour into 2 buttered 9-inch cake pans. Sprinkle the pecans over the top. Prepare the cake mix using the package directions. Pour the batter over the pecans. Bake at 325 degrees for 35 to 45 minutes or until the cake tests done. Cool in the pans for 10 minutes. Invert onto wire racks to cool completely.

Beat the whipping cream in a bowl until soft peaks form. Add the confectioners' sugar and vanilla and beat until stiff peaks form. Place a cake layer pecan side up on a serving plate. Spread with half the whipped cream mixture. Top with the second cake layer, pecan side up. Spread with the remaining whipped cream mixture. Garnish with chocolate curls.

Serves 8 to 10

German Chocolate Upside-Down Cake

1 cup shredded coconut
1 cup chopped pecans
1 (2-layer) package German
    chocolate cake mix

8 ounces cream cheese
1/2 cup (1 stick) margarine
1 (1-pound) package confectioners'
    sugar

Sprinkle the coconut and pecans in the bottom of a 9x13-inch cake pan. Prepare the cake mix using the package directions and pour into the prepared pan. Heat the cream cheese and margarine in a saucepan over medium heat until blended, stirring constantly. Remove from the heat and blend in the confectioners' sugar. Spoon over the cake batter. Bake at 350 degrees for 35 to 40 minutes. Cool on a wire rack. Cut into serving portions. Invert each portion onto a dessert plate.

Serves 15

Gooey Cake

1 (2-layer) package German
    chocolate cake mix
1 (14-ounce) can sweetened
    condensed milk

1 (16-ounce) jar butterscotch or
    caramel ice cream topping
12 ounces whipped topping
3 Heath or Skor candy bars, frozen

Prepare and bake the cake mix using the package directions in a 9x13-inch cake pan. Pierce the warm cake with a wooden spoon handle halfway into the cake at 1-inch intervals. Pour the condensed milk into the holes. Spread with the ice cream topping. Chill until set. Spread with the whipped topping. Crush the frozen candy bars and sprinkle over the top. Chill, covered, for 8 to 10 hours.

Serves 15

Mocha Party Cake

1 (16-ounce) package angel food
   cake mix
3/4 cup chocolate chips
1/2 teaspoon instant coffee powder
2 tablespoons water

4 eggs, separated
1/4 cup sugar
1 teaspoon ground cinnamon
1/4 teaspoon ground cloves
1 cup whipping cream, whipped

Prepare and bake the cake mix using the package directions. Invert onto a funnel to cool. Combine the chocolate chips, coffee powder and water in a double boiler. Heat over hot water until blended, stirring constantly. Remove from the heat. Cool slightly. Add the egg yolks 1 at a time, beating well after each addition.

Beat the egg whites in a large bowl until foamy. Add the sugar and spices gradually, beating until stiff. Fold the chocolate mixture into the stiffly beaten egg whites. Fold in the whipped cream.

Cut the cake into 3 layers. Spread the chocolate mixture between the layers and over the top and side of the cake. Chill for 4 hours or longer.

Serves 12

Cappuccino Cake

1/3 cup semisweet chocolate chips
1/3 cup chopped hazelnuts
1 (2-layer) package yellow cake mix
2 teaspoons cinnamon
1 1/4 cups water
1 egg
1/2 cup egg substitute

1/3 cup double-strength coffee or
   espresso, cooled
2 tablespoons instant coffee powder
   or espresso roast
Confectioners' sugar
Cinnamon

Spray a bundt pan with nonstick cooking spray and lightly dust with flour. Sprinkle the chocolate chips and hazelnuts evenly over the bottom of the pan. Combine the cake mix and cinnamon in a bowl and mix well. Add the water, egg, egg substitute and cooled coffee and beat at low speed until moistened. Beat at medium speed for 2 minutes. Pour into the prepared pan. Sprinkle with the coffee powder and swirl into the batter with a knife.

Bake at 325 degrees for 35 to 45 minutes or until a wooden pick inserted in the center comes out clean. Cool on a wire rack for 15 minutes. Remove to a serving plate to cool completely. Sprinkle with confectioners' sugar and cinnamon.

Serves 12

Toasted Coconut Cake

Cake

1 (2-layer) package white cake mix
1 (3-ounce) package vanilla instant
   pudding mix
1 1/3 cups water

1/4 cup vegetable oil
4 eggs
1 1/3 cups flaked coconut
1 cup chopped pecans

Toasted Coconut Cream Cheese Frosting

2 tablespoons butter
2 1/2 cups flaked coconut
2 tablespoons butter, softened
8 ounces cream cheese, softened

3 1/2 cups sifted confectioners' sugar
2 teaspoons milk
1/2 teaspoon vanilla extract

For the cake, combine the cake mix, pudding mix, water, oil and eggs in a mixing bowl and beat at medium speed for 4 minutes. Stir in the coconut and pecans. Pour into 3 greased and floured 9-inch cake pans. Bake at 350 degrees for 20 to 25 minutes or until the layers test done. Cool in the pans for 10 minutes. Invert onto a wire rack to cool completely.

For the frosting, melt 2 tablespoons butter in a large skillet. Stir in the coconut. Cook over medium heat until golden brown, stirring constantly. Remove from the heat and let stand until cool. Combine 2 tablespoons butter and the cream cheese in a bowl and beat until light and fluffy. Add the confectioners' sugar, milk and vanilla and beat until smooth. Reserve 1/2 cup toasted coconut. Stir the remaining coconut into the frosting. Spread the frosting between the layers and over the top and side of the cake. Sprinkle with the reserved coconut.

Serves 12

Graham Streusel Cake

2 cups graham cracker crumbs
3/4 cup packed brown sugar
3/4 cup melted butter
1 1/4 teaspoons cinnamon
1 (2-layer) package yellow cake mix

1 cup water
1/4 cup vegetable oil
3 eggs
1 cup confectioners' sugar
1 to 2 tablespoons water

Mix the graham cracker crumbs, brown sugar, butter and cinnamon in a bowl. Combine the cake mix, 1 cup water, oil and eggs in a bowl and mix well. Layer the cake batter and crumb mixture 1/2 at a time in a greased and floured 9x13-inch cake pan. Bake at 350 degrees for 45 minutes. Drizzle the warm cake with a mixture of the confectioners' sugar and 1 to 2 tablespoons water.

Serves 15

Honey Bun Cake

1 (2-layer) package yellow cake mix
1/2 cup sugar
2/3 cup vegetable oil
4 eggs
1 cup sour cream

1/2 cup packed brown sugar
2 teaspoons cinnamon
1 cup confectioners' sugar
1/4 cup milk

Combine the cake mix, sugar, oil, eggs and sour cream in a mixing bowl and mix well. Combine the brown sugar and cinnamon in a small bowl and mix well. Pour half the batter into a greased 9x13-inch cake pan. Sprinkle half the cinnamon mixture over the batter. Add the remaining batter. Sprinkle with the remaining cinnamon mixture. Swirl back and forth with a knife. Bake at 350 degrees for 35 minutes. Combine the confectioners' sugar and milk in a bowl and mix well. Pour over the warm cake.

Serves 15

Ice Cream Cake

1 (2-layer) package white cake mix
2 cups cherry ice cream (or flavor of
   choice), melted
3 eggs

$1/3$ (16-ounce) can fudge frosting
$1/3$ (16-ounce) can white frosting
$1/3$ (16-ounce) can cherry frosting

Spray a bundt pan lightly with nonstick cooking spray and dust with flour. Combine the cake mix, melted ice cream and eggs in a large mixing bowl and beat at low speed for 1 minute, scraping the side of the bowl. Beat at medium speed for 2 minutes. Pour into the prepared bundt pan, smoothing the surface with a rubber spatula.

Bake at 350 degrees for 38 to 42 minutes or until the cake begins to pull away from the side of the pan and the top springs back when lightly touched. Cool in the pan for 20 minutes. Invert onto a wire rack to cool completely.

Microwave the fudge frosting in a microwave-safe bowl on High for 15 to 20 seconds. Drizzle over the cooled cake. Repeat the procedure with the white frosting and cherry frosting.

Serves 16

Jack-O'-Lantern Cake

2 (2-layer) packages yellow or
  chocolate cake mixes
3 cups confectioners' sugar
1/2 cup (1 stick) butter or margarine,
  softened

1 1/2 teaspoons vanilla extract
2 tablespoons (about) milk
Green food coloring
Red and yellow food coloring
1 (10-ounce) chocolate candy bar

Prepare the cake mixes using the package directions. Remove enough batter to make
1 cupcake. Bake the cakes at 350 degrees in bundt pans as directed, baking the cupcake
batter in a muffin tin.

Combine the confectioners' sugar, butter, vanilla and 1 tablespoon of the milk in a bowl
and mix well. Stir in the remaining tablespoon of milk gradually until the frosting is easy
to spread but not runny. Remove enough frosting to frost the cupcake. Stir green food
coloring into the small amount of frosting. Add red and yellow food coloring to the
remaining frosting to make it orange.

Place 1 bundt cake upside down on a serving plate and frost with the orange frosting.
Place the second cake right side up over the first and frost with the orange frosting. Place
the cupcake in the center of the cake, coating it with the green frosting. Cut the candy
bar into small triangles and arrange them on the side of the cake to make the eyes, nose
and mouth of the jack-o'-lantern. When ready to serve, slice the top cake first, then the
bottom one.

Serves 32 to 36

Peanut Crunch Cake

1 (2-layer) package yellow cake mix
1 cup peanut butter
1/2 cup packed light brown sugar
1 cup water
3 eggs

1/4 cup vegetable oil
1/2 to 3/4 cup semisweet chocolate chips
1/2 to 3/4 cup peanut butter chips
1/2 cup chopped peanuts

Combine the cake mix, peanut butter and brown sugar in a mixing bowl and beat at low speed until crumbly. Reserve 1/2 cup of the mixture. Add the water, eggs and oil to the remaining crumb mixture and beat at low speed until moistened. Beat at high speed for 2 minutes. Stir in 1/4 cup each of the chocolate and peanut butter chips. Pour into a greased 9x13-inch baking pan. Combine the peanuts, reserved crumb mixture and remaining chips and sprinkle over the batter. Bake at 350 degrees for 40 to 45 minutes or until a wooden pick inserted near the center comes out clean. Let cool completely.

Serves 12 to 16

Pistachio Pudding Cake

1 (2-layer) package white cake mix
4 cups milk

2 (4-ounce) packages pistachio instant pudding mix

Prepare and bake the cake mix using the package directions in a 9x13-inch cake pan. Poke holes in the cake using the round handle of a wooden spoon at 1-inch intervals. Whisk together the milk and pudding mix in a bowl for 2 minutes. Pour half the pudding mixture evenly over the warm cake. Chill the remaining pudding mixture until slightly thickened. Spoon over the top of the cake, swirling to frost. Chill, covered, for 1 hour before serving. Store the cake, covered, in the refrigerator.

Serves 15

Peanut Butter Cream Cookie Cake

1 (2-layer) package white cake mix
1 cup water
1/3 cup vegetable oil
2 eggs
1 1/4 cups coarsely crushed peanut
   butter sandwich cookies

1 (16-ounce) can vanilla frosting
1/2 cup creamy peanut butter
2 tablespoons milk
1/2 cup coarsely crushed peanut
   butter sandwich cookies

Combine the cake mix, water, oil and eggs in a mixing bowl and beat at low speed until moistened. Beat at high speed for 2 minutes. Fold in 1 1/4 cups crushed cookies. Spoon into a greased 9x13-inch cake pan. Bake at 350 degrees for 30 to 40 minutes or until the cake tests done. Remove to a wire rack to cool completely. Combine the frosting, peanut butter and milk in a mixing bowl and beat until smooth. Spread evenly over the cooled cake. Sprinkle with 1/2 cup crushed cookies.

Serves 16

Pistachio Poppy Seed Cake

1 (2-layer) package yellow cake mix
1/2 cup warm water
1/2 cup milk
5 eggs

2 (4-ounce) packages pistachio
   instant pudding mix
2 tablespoons flour
1/2 cup poppy seeds

Combine the cake mix, water, milk, eggs, pudding mix, flour and poppy seeds in a bowl and mix well. Spoon into a greased and floured bundt pan. Bake at 375 degrees for 40 to 45 minutes or until the cake tests done. Cool in the pan for 10 minutes. Invert onto a serving plate.

Serves 15

Praline Cake

1 (2-layer) package yellow cake mix
1/2 cup sugar
1/2 cup vegetable oil
1 cup milk
3 eggs
1/2 cup (1 stick) margarine, softened

2 eggs
1 (1-pound) package light brown
  sugar
2 tablespoons flour
1 teaspoon vanilla extract
1 1/2 cups coarsely chopped pecans

Combine the cake mix, sugar, oil and milk in mixing bowl and beat well. Add 3 eggs 1 at a time, beating well after each addition. Pour into a greased 8x12-inch cake pan.

Combine the margarine, 2 eggs, brown sugar and flour in a mixing bowl and beat well. Stir in the vanilla and pecans. Spread over the top of the batter. Bake at 350 degrees for 30 minutes.

Serves 16

**Unfrosted cakes will keep up to 6 months in the freezer.
Let the cake cool completely before freezing. Thaw the cake, wrapped,
at room temperature for 2 to 3 hours.**

Maple Pumpkin Spice Cake

Cake
1 (2-layer) package spice cake mix
2 eggs, unbeaten
1 (15-ounce) can pumpkin

3/4 cup water
2 tablespoons maple syrup
1/4 teaspoon baking soda

Buttercream Frosting
3 tablespoons flour
3/4 cup milk
1/2 cup (1 stick) butter or margarine,
   softened

1/2 cup shortening
1 teaspoon vanilla extract
3/4 cup sugar

For the cake, combine the cake mix, eggs, pumpkin, water, maple syrup and baking soda in a bowl and mix well. Pour into a greased and floured 9x13-inch baking dish or 2 greased and floured 8-inch round cake pans. Bake at 350 degrees for 30 to 35 minutes or until the cake tests done. Cool in the pan for 10 minutes. Remove to a wire rack to cool completely.

For the frosting, combine the flour and milk in a saucepan over medium heat. Cook until thickened, stirring constantly. Remove from the heat and let stand until cool. Cream the butter, shortening, vanilla and sugar in a mixing bowl until light and fluffy. Beat in the flour mixture. Beat until the consistency of whipped cream. Frost the cooled cake.

Serves 12 to 15

Pumpkin Upside-Down Cake

3 eggs, lightly beaten
1 (29-ounce) can pumpkin
1 1/2 cups sugar
1 (12-ounce) can evaporated milk
2 teaspoons cinnamon

1 teaspoon nutmeg
1/2 teaspoon ginger
1 (2-layer) package yellow cake mix
3/4 cup margarine, melted
1 cup chopped walnuts

Combine the eggs, pumpkin, sugar, evaporated milk, cinnamon, nutmeg and ginger in a bowl and mix well. Spoon into an ungreased 9x13-inch cake pan. Sprinkle with the cake mix. Drizzle with the melted margarine. Bake at 350 degrees for 30 minutes. Press the walnuts gently into the baked layer. Bake for 30 minutes longer or until brown. Let stand until cool. Serve with whipped cream.

Serves 14

Sunflower Cake

For a fun summertime treat, try making this sunflower cake. Prepare and bake a yellow cake mix using the package directions for two 9-inch round pans. Place one of the layers on a large round tray and arrange Twinkies around the cake to form the petals. Add enough yellow food coloring to your favorite homemade or canned white frosting to make the bright yellow of sunflower petals. Frost the cake and Twinkies. Arrange chocolate chips in the center of the cake to emulate sunflower seeds. This is especially spectacular if the chocolate chips are carefully spiraled from the center as the seeds are naturally. Use the other cake layer for another sunflower, or eat as desired.

Easy Red Velvet Cake

Cake

1 (2-layer) package yellow cake mix
Buttermilk
2 tablespoons baking cocoa

1 (1-ounce) bottle of red food
 coloring

Vanilla Cream Frosting

1/2 cup flour
1 cup milk
Pinch of salt
1/2 cup margarine, softened

1/2 cup shortening
1 cup sugar
2 teaspoons vanilla extract

For the cake, prepare the cake mix using the package directions, substituting buttermilk for water. Stir the baking cocoa and food coloring into the batter. Pour into a greased and floured 9x13-inch cake pan. Bake using the package directions.

For the frosting, combine the flour, milk and salt in a saucepan. Cook until thickened, stirring constantly. Remove from the heat and let stand until cool. Cream the margarine, shortening, sugar and vanilla in a mixing bowl until light and fluffy. Stir into the flour mixture. Beat at high speed until of spreading consistency. Spread over the cooled cake.

Serves 20 to 24

Ricotta Cake

Cake

1 (2-layer) package butter-recipe
  yellow cake mix
1 (15-ounce) container ricotta
  cheese

3 eggs
2 teaspoons vanilla extract
3/4 cup sugar

Cream Cheese Topping

1 (4-ounce) package vanilla
  pudding mix
1 cup milk
1 (8-ounce) package cream cheese,
  softened
1 (8-ounce) container whipped
  topping

1 (15-ounce) can crushed pineapple,
  drained
Coconut (optional)
Chopped walnuts or pecans
  (optional)

For the cake, grease and flour a 9x13-inch cake pan. Prepare the cake mix using the package directions. Pour into the prepared pan. Beat the ricotta, eggs, vanilla and sugar together in a bowl. Pour over the cake batter. Bake at 350 degrees for 55 minutes or until the cake tests done. Cool completely.

For the topping, prepare the pudding with the milk using the package directions. Beat the cream cheese in a bowl until light and fluffy. Fold in the whipped topping and pudding. Spread the topping over the cake. Top with the pineapple. Sprinkle with coconut and walnuts.

Serves 8 to 10

Upside-Down Spice Cake

1/2 cup sugar
1/4 cup orange juice
2 teaspoons grated orange zest
1/4 cup flaked coconut
1 (15-ounce) can pear halves,
    drained, 3/4 cup syrup reserved

1 (2-layer) package spice cake mix
3/4 cup orange juice
1/4 teaspoon salt
1 tablespoon butter
2 tablespoons cornstarch

Combine the sugar, 1/4 cup orange juice, the orange zest and coconut in a bowl and mix well. Pour into a buttered 8-inch square cake pan. Arrange the pears over the sugar mixture, cut side down. Prepare the cake mix using the package directions. Pour evenly over the pears. Bake at 350 degrees for 30 to 35 minutes or until the cake tests done.

Combine the reserved pear syrup, 3/4 cup orange juice, salt, butter and cornstarch in a small saucepan over low heat to make the orange sauce. Cook for 3 minutes or until thickened, stirring constantly. Remove from the heat. Remove the cake from the oven and let cool in the pan for 10 minutes. Invert onto a serving plate. Serve with the orange sauce and/or whipped topping.

Serves 6

White Turtle Cake

Cake

1 (2-layer) package yellow cake mix
1 cup water
1 (14-ounce) can sweetened
   condensed milk

1 cup vegetable oil
3 eggs
1 (14-ounce) package caramels
1 cup chopped pecans

White Turtle Frosting

$^1/_2$ cup (1 stick) margarine, melted
1 (1-pound) package confectioners'
   sugar

6 tablespoons milk
1 teaspoon vanilla extract

For the cake, combine the cake mix, water, half the condensed milk, oil and eggs in a mixing bowl and beat well. Pour half the batter evenly into a greased 9x13-inch cake pan. Bake at 350 degrees for 30 minutes. Melt the caramels with the remaining condensed milk in a saucepan, stirring frequently. Stir in pecans. Pour over the hot cake. Spread the remaining batter over the caramel layer. Bake for 20 minutes longer.

For the frosting, combine the margarine, confectioners' sugar and milk in a mixing bowl and beat well. Add the vanilla and mix well. Spread the frosting over the warm cake.

Serves 12

Black Walnut Cake

Cake
1 (2-layer) package white cake mix

1 cup chopped black walnuts

Black Walnut Frosting
1 cup packed dark brown sugar

$1/2$ cup (1 stick) butter

$1/4$ cup milk

$2^1/2$ cups confectioners' sugar

$3/4$ cup chopped black walnuts

For the cake, prepare and bake the cake mix with 1 cup chopped walnuts using the package directions for two 9-inch cake pans. Cool in the pans for several minutes. Remove to a wire rack to cool completely.

For the frosting, combine the brown sugar and butter in a saucepan. Boil for 2 minutes, stirring constantly. Add the milk. Bring to a boil, stirring constantly. Remove from the heat and let cool completely. Add the confectioners' sugar and beat until smooth and creamy. Stir in the walnuts. Spread between the layers and over the top and side of the cooled cake.

Serves 20

Watergate Cake

Cake

1 (2-layer) package white cake mix
1 cup vegetable oil
3 eggs, beaten
1 cup club soda

1 (4-ounce) package pistachio
   instant pudding mix
1/2 cup chopped pecans

Pistachio Cream Frosting

1 cup milk
1 cup confectioners' sugar
16 ounces whipped topping
1 cup sour cream

1 (4-ounce) package pistachio
   instant pudding mix
1/2 cup chopped pecans

For the cake, combine the cake mix, oil and eggs in a mixing bowl and mix well. Add the club soda, pudding mix and pecans and beat for 4 minutes. Pour into 2 greased and floured 8-inch cake pans. Bake at 325 degrees for 30 minutes or until the layers test done. Cool in the pans for 10 minutes. Remove to a wire rack to cool completely. Invert onto a cake plate.

For the frosting, combine the milk, confectioners' sugar, whipped topping and sour cream in a mixing bowl and beat until smooth. Add the pudding mix and beat until stiff peaks form. Fold in the pecans. Frost the cooled cake. Store, covered, in the refrigerator.

Serves 12

Saucy Apple Swirl Cake

1/4 cup sugar
2 teaspoons cinnamon
1 (2-layer) package yellow cake mix

1 2/3 cups applesauce
3 eggs

Combine the sugar and cinnamon in a small bowl. Butter a 10-inch tube pan or bundt pan and dust with 1 teaspoon of the cinnamon mixture. Combine the cake mix, applesauce and eggs in a large bowl and beat as directed on the cake mix package. Pour into the prepared pan, reserving 1 1/2 cups of the batter. Sprinkle with the cinnamon mixture. Top with the reserved batter. Swirl the remaining cinnamon mixture through the batter with a knife or spatula. Bake at 350 degrees for 35 to 45 minutes or until cake tests done. Cool in the pan for 15 minutes. Invert onto a serving plate.

Serves 12

Apple Pumpkin Cake

1 (2-layer) package spice cake mix
1/2 cup water
3 eggs

1 cup applesauce
1 (15-ounce) can pumpkin

Combine the cake mix, water and eggs in a mixing bowl and mix well. Add the applesauce and pumpkin and mix well. Spoon into a 9x13-inch cake pan. Bake at 350 degrees for 30 to 35 minutes or until a wooden pick inserted near the center comes out clean. Cool in the pan.

Serves 12

Apricot Nectar Cake with Lemon Glaze

Cake

1 (2-layer) package yellow cake mix
1 small package lemon gelatin or
    pudding mix
1 cup apricot nectar

3/4 cup vegetable oil
4 eggs
1 teaspoon vanilla extract

Lemon Glaze

1 cup sifted confectioners' sugar

Lemon juice to taste

For the cake, combine the cake mix and gelatin in a mixing bowl and mix well. Add the apricot nectar and oil. Beat for 4 to 5 minutes, scraping the bowl occasionally. Add the eggs 1 at a time, beating well after each addition. Beat in the vanilla. Spoon into a greased and floured tube pan.

Bake at 325 degrees for 1 hour or until the cake tests done. Cool in the pan for 10 minutes. Invert onto a wire rack to cool completely.

For the glaze, combine the confectioners' sugar and lemon juice in a small bowl, stirring until of glaze consistency. Drizzle over cake.

Serves 16

Banana Fudge Ring

Cake

1 (2-layer) package chocolate fudge
   cake mix
1 (4-ounce) package chocolate
   instant pudding mix

4 eggs
1 cup water
1/2 cup mashed banana
1/4 cup vegetable oil

Banana Cream Frosting

1 package buttercream milk
   chocolate frosting mix
2 cups whipping cream

1/2 cup mashed banana
1/2 cup chopped pecans

For the cake, combine the cake mix, pudding mix and eggs in a mixing bowl and mix well. Add the water, banana and oil. Beat at medium speed for 8 minutes. Spoon the batter into a greased and lightly floured 10-inch tube pan.

Bake at 350 degrees for 45 to 50 minutes or until the cake tests done. Cool in the pan for 15 minutes. Invert onto a serving plate.

For the frosting, combine the frosting mix and whipping cream in a mixing bowl and beat until thickened. Add the banana and mix well. Stir in the pecans. Spread the frosting over the side and top of the cake. Chill until serving time.

Serves 12

Banana Crunch Cake

5 tablespoons margarine, melted
1 package coconut-pecan frosting
  mix
1 cup rolled oats

1 cup sour cream
4 eggs, beaten
1 1/2 bananas, chopped
1 (2-layer) package yellow cake mix

Combine the margarine and frosting mix in a small bowl and mix well. Cut in the oats until crumbly. Combine the sour cream, eggs and bananas in a large mixing bowl. Stir in the cake mix. Beat for 2 minutes. Layer the batter and crumb mixture 1/3 at a time in a greased and floured 10-inch tube pan. Bake at 350 degrees for 40 minutes or until the cake tests done. Cool upright in the pan for 15 minutes. Place crumb side up on a serving plate.

Serves 16

Busy Day Jam Cake

1 (2-layer) package spice cake mix
1 (4-ounce) package vanilla instant
  pudding mix
1 1/4 cups blackberry jam
3/4 cup water

1/4 cup vegetable oil
4 eggs
1 cup raisins
1 cup chopped black walnuts
2 tablespoons flour

Combine the cake mix, pudding mix, jam, water, oil and eggs in a mixing bowl. Beat at medium speed for 4 minutes, scraping the bowl occasionally. Fold in a mixture of the raisins, black walnuts and flour. Spoon into 3 greased and floured 9-inch cake pans. Bake at 350 degrees for 30 minutes or until the layers test done. Cool in the pans for 5 minutes. Remove to a wire rack to cool completely. Spread your favorite caramel frosting between the layers and over the top and side of the cake.

Serves 12

Key Lime Cake

Cake
1 (2-layer) package lemon cake mix
1 (3-ounce) package lemon instant
   pudding mix
1 cup egg substitute or 4 eggs

1/2 cup water
1/2 cup vegetable oil
1/2 cup Key lime juice

Key Lime Glaze
1 cup confectioners' sugar

2 tablespoons Key lime juice

For the cake, combine the cake mix, pudding mix, egg substitute, water, oil and Key lime juice in a mixing bowl. Beat for 2 minutes at medium speed. Pour the batter into a greased and floured 9x13-inch cake pan. Bake at 350 degrees for 35 minutes or until a wooden pick inserted in the center comes out clean. Cool in the pan on a wire rack.

For the glaze, combine the confectioners' sugar and Key lime juice in a bowl and mix well, adding additional juice if needed. Drizzle over the cake. Cut into squares.

Serves 15 to 18

When packing a piece of frosted one-layer cake in your child's lunch box, cut the slice into halves horizontally and place the bottom half on top of the frosting to make a sandwich. Now the frosting will not stick to the wrap.

Lemon Cream Cake

1 (2-layer) package pudding-recipe
   lemon cake mix
2 (14-ounce) cans sweetened
   condensed milk

$2/3$ cup lemon juice
8 ounces whipped topping

Prepare and bake the cake mix using the package directions for two 8-inch cake pans. Cool as directed. Mix half the condensed milk and half the lemon juice in a bowl. Spread between the cake layers. Mix the remaining condensed milk, remaining lemon juice and the whipped topping in a bowl. Spread over the top and side of the cake. Chill, covered, until ready to serve.

Serves 12

Lemon-Glazed Cake

1 (2-layer) package lemon cake mix
1 (4-ounce) package lemon instant
   pudding mix
$1/2$ cup vegetable oil
$3/4$ cup water

4 eggs
2 cups confectioners' sugar
2 tablespoons butter
$1/3$ cup fresh lemon juice
2 tablespoons water

Combine the cake mix, pudding mix, oil, $3/4$ cup water and eggs in a mixing bowl. Beat at medium speed for 4 minutes. Spoon into a greased and floured 9x13-inch cake pan. Bake at 350 degrees for 30 to 40 minutes or until the cake tests done. Blend the confectioners' sugar, butter, lemon juice and 2 tablespoons water in a bowl. Pierce holes in the cake with a fork. Pour the glaze over the hot cake. Let stand until cool.

Serves 15

Favorite Lemon Pudding Cake

1 (2-layer) package yellow cake mix
1 (4-ounce) package lemon instant
  pudding mix
1 cup orange juice

1/2 cup vegetable oil
4 eggs
1 cup sugar
2/3 cup orange juice

Combine the cake mix, pudding mix, 1 cup orange juice, oil and eggs in a mixing bowl and mix until moistened. Beat at medium speed for 2 minutes. Pour into a tube pan sprayed with nonstick cooking spray. Bake at 350 degrees for 55 to 60 minutes or until the cake tests done. Cool in the pan for 5 minutes. Invert onto a cake plate. Combine the sugar and 2/3 cup orange juice in a bowl and mix well. Pour over the cake.

Serves 16

Orange Juice Cake

1/2 cup chopped pecans
1 (2-layer) package yellow butter
  cake mix
1 (4-ounce) package vanilla instant
  pudding mix
1 cup orange juice

1/2 cup vegetable oil
4 eggs
1 cup sugar
1/4 cup orange juice
1/2 cup (1 stick) margarine

Grease and flour a bundt pan. Sprinkle with the pecans. Combine the cake mix, pudding mix, 1 cup orange juice, oil and eggs in a bowl and mix well. Pour into the prepared pan. Bake at 350 degrees for 50 to 60 minutes or until the cake tests done. Bring the sugar, 1/4 cup orange juice and margarine to a boil in a saucepan. Cook for 2 minutes, stirring frequently. Pour over the hot cake. Let stand for 30 minutes. Invert onto a cake platter.

Serves 12

Tropical Orange Cake

1 (2-layer) package white cake mix
1 cup water
2 eggs
1 (14-ounce) can sweetened
   condensed milk

2 teaspoons grated orange peel
1 (3-ounce) can flaked coconut
   (1 1/3 cups)
1/4 cup thawed frozen orange juice
   concentrate

Combine the cake mix, water, eggs, 1/3 cup of the condensed milk and the orange peel in a mixing bowl. Beat at low speed until moistened. Beat at high speed for 3 minutes. Stir in 1 cup of the coconut. Pour into a greased and floured 9x13-inch cake pan. Bake at 350 degrees for 30 minutes. Cool in the pan on a wire rack. Combine the remaining condensed milk, remaining coconut and orange juice concentrate in a bowl and mix well. Spread over the cool cake. Chill, covered, in the refrigerator.

Serves 15

Pineapple Cake

1 (1-layer) package white or yellow
   cake mix
1 (4-ounce) package vanilla, French
   vanilla or pineapple instant
   pudding mix

2 cups milk
8 ounces cream cheese, softened
1 (20-ounce) can crushed pineapple,
   drained
8 ounces whipped topping

Prepare the cake mix using the package directions. Pour into a nonstick 9x13-inch cake pan. Bake at 350 degrees until the cake tests done. Beat the pudding mix with the milk in a mixing bowl until the mixture begins to thicken. Add the cream cheese and mix well. Pour over the baked layer. Sprinkle the pineapple over the top. Spread with the whipped topping. Chill, covered, for several hours.

Serves 15

Tropical Dream Cake

Cake

1 (2-layer) package yellow cake mix
   with pudding
1 cup water or pineapple juice
1/3 cup vegetable oil

3 eggs
1 (14-ounce) can sweetened
   condensed milk
1 teaspoon coconut extract

Pineapple Topping

1 (15-ounce) can crushed pineapple,
   drained
1 (3-ounce) package vanilla or
   coconut cream instant
   pudding mix

8 ounces cream cheese, softened
1 teaspoon coconut extract
8 ounces whipped topping

For the cake, combine the cake mix, water, oil and eggs in a large bowl. Beat for 2 minutes at high speed. Pour into a greased 9x13-inch cake pan.

Bake at 350 degrees for 25 to 35 minutes or until the cake tests done. Cool for 5 minutes. Pierce the top with a fork every 1 to 2 inches. Pour a mixture of the condensed milk and coconut extract slowly over the top. Chill for 2 hours or longer.

For the topping, combine the pineapple, pudding mix, cream cheese and coconut extract in a bowl and mix until of the desired spreading consistency. Spread evenly over the chilled cake just before serving. Top with whipped topping.

Serves 15

Strawberry Cake

Cake

1 (18-ounce) package white cake mix
1 (3-ounce) package strawberry
  gelatin
1 cup shortening
4 eggs

1/2 cup milk
1/2 cup frozen strawberries, thawed
  and crushed
1/2 cup flaked coconut
1/2 cup chopped pecans

Strawberry Frosting

1 (16-ounce) package
  confectioners' sugar
1/3 cup melted margarine

1/2 cup chopped pecans
1/2 cup strawberry purée
1/2 cup flaked coconut

For the cake, combine the cake mix, gelatin, shortening, eggs, milk, strawberries, coconut and pecans in a mixing bowl. Beat for 2 minutes. Pour into 3 greased 9-inch cake pans.

Bake at 350 degrees until the cakes test done. Cool in the pans for 10 minutes. Remove to a wire rack to cool completely.

For the frosting, beat the confectioners' sugar and margarine in a bowl until light and fluffy. Add the pecans, strawberry purée and coconut and mix well. Spread between the layers and over the top and side of the cake.

Serves 8

Peachy Strawberry Cake

1 (2-layer) package yellow cake mix
16 ounces whipped topping
1 teaspoon vanilla extract

1 (16-ounce) can sliced peaches,
  drained
2 cups sliced strawberries

Prepare and bake the cake using the package directions for 2 layers. Cool in the pans for 10 minutes. Remove to a wire rack to cool completely. Combine the whipped topping and vanilla in a bowl and mix well. Spread 1/4 of the whipped topping on 1 cake layer. Arrange the peaches and sliced strawberries on the prepared layer. Top with the remaining layer. Spread the remaining whipped topping over the top and side of the cake. Garnish with whole strawberries.

Serves 16

Elegant Party Cake

1 (2-layer) package yellow
  cake mix
1 1/2 cups plain yogurt
1 (6-ounce) can frozen lemonade
  concentrate, thawed

1 (14-ounce) can sweetened
  condensed milk
1 pint fresh strawberries or
  raspberries, sliced
4 kiwifruit, peeled and sliced

Prepare and bake the cake mix using the package directions for two 9-inch cake pans. Remove to a wire rack to cool. Split the layers horizontally into halves. Combine the yogurt, lemonade concentrate and condensed milk in a bowl and mix well. Spread 1/4 of the mixture over 1 cake layer. Stack the cake layers with fruit between, alternating kiwifruit and strawberries and spreading 1/4 of the lemonade mixture over each cake layer. The mixture will run down the side of cake. Decorate the top of the cake with concentric rings of remaining fruit. Chill until serving time.

Serves 10 to 12

Friendship Fruit

3¹/₂ cups sugar
1¹/₂ cups mixed fruit juices
1 (28-ounce) can sliced peaches
1 (20-ounce) can crushed pineapple

3¹/₂ cups sugar
1 (20-ounce) can fruit cocktail
2 (9-ounce) jars maraschino
   cherries, drained

Combine 3¹/₂ cups sugar, fruit juices and undrained peaches in a glass bowl. Let stand, tightly covered, at room temperature for 10 days, stirring every 24 hours. Add the undrained pineapple, 3¹/₂ cups sugar and fruit cocktail. Let stand for 10 days, stirring every 24 hours. Add the cherries. Let stand for 10 days longer, stirring every 24 hours. Drain the fruit, reserving the liquid. Use the fruit in cake, over ice cream or as gifts for friends. Substitute reserved liquid for the mixed fruit juices to make additional recipes of Friendship Fruit.

Makes 4¹/₂ cups

Friendship Cake

1 (18-ounce) package yellow
   cake mix
1 (6-ounce) package vanilla instant
   pudding mix
2/3 cup vegetable oil

4 eggs
1 cup raisins
1 cup coconut
1 cup chopped pecans
1¹/₂ cups Friendship Fruit

Combine the cake mix, pudding mix, oil and eggs in a mixing bowl. Beat at medium speed for 4 minutes. Fold in the raisins, coconut, pecans and Friendship Fruit. Pour into a greased and floured bundt pan. Bake at 350 degrees for 40 to 60 minutes or until the cake tests done. Cool in the pan for 10 minutes. Invert onto a wire rack to cool completely.

Serves 16

Fruit Cocktail Cake

Cake
1 (2-layer) package yellow cake mix
2 eggs

1 (17-ounce) can fruit cocktail
1/2 cup chopped English walnuts

Pineapple Topping
1 (16-ounce) can crushed pineapple
1 (4-ounce) package lemon instant
   pudding mix

8 ounces whipped topping
1/2 cup chopped English walnuts

For the cake, combine the cake mix, eggs, undrained fruit cocktail and walnuts in a mixing bowl. Beat for 30 seconds or until moistened. Beat at medium speed for 2 minutes. Pour into a greased and floured 11x17-inch cake pan. Bake at 375 degrees for 30 minutes. Let stand until cool.

For the topping, combine the pineapple, pudding mix and whipped topping in a bowl. Spread over the cooled cake. Sprinkle with the walnuts. Chill until serving time.

Serves 24

Make an easy frozen dessert of torn angel food cake and softened coffee ice cream. Freeze in a loaf pan lined with waxed paper and serve sliced with chocolate sauce.

Fruity Pudding Cake

Cake

1 (2-layer) package yellow cake mix
1 (4-ounce) package lemon instant
  pudding mix
1 (16-ounce) can fruit cocktail
1 cup flaked coconut

4 eggs
$1/4$ cup vegetable oil
$1/2$ cup packed brown sugar
$1/2$ cup chopped pecans

Coconut Glaze

$1/2$ cup (1 stick) butter
$1/2$ cup sugar

$1/2$ cup evaporated milk
$1^1/2$ cups flaked coconut

For the cake, combine the cake mix, pudding mix, undrained fruit cocktail, coconut, eggs and oil in a mixing bowl. Beat at medium speed for 4 minutes. Spoon into a greased and floured 9x13-inch cake pan. Sprinkle with the brown sugar and pecans. Bake at 325 degrees for 45 minutes. Cool in the pan for 15 minutes.

For the glaze, bring the butter, sugar and evaporated milk to a boil in a saucepan. Boil for 2 minutes. Stir in the coconut. Pour over the warm cake.

Serves 15

Cookies,
Cookies,
Cookies

Chewy Treasure Cookies

1 (2-layer) package cake mix
  of choice
2/3 cup butter-flavor shortening
3 eggs
1 teaspoon poppy seeds (optional)
1 cup raisins (optional)

1 cup chopped walnuts or pecans
  (optional)
1 cup chocolate chips (optional)
1 cup peanut butter chips (optional)
1 cup shredded coconut (optional)

Combine the cake mix, shortening and eggs in a large mixing bowl and beat until smooth. Stir in the optional ingredients of your choice. Drop by rounded teaspoonfuls 2 inches apart onto a buttered cookie sheet.

Bake at 350 degrees for 10 to 11 minutes or until the edges are firm. Cool on the cookie sheet for 2 minutes. Remove to a wire rack to cool completely.

Makes about 3 dozen cookies

Cherry Drop Cookies

1 (2-layer) package cherry cake mix
1/4 cup vegetable oil
2 tablespoons water
2 eggs

Red food coloring (optional)
1 cup chopped pecans
Maraschino cherries, quartered

Combine the cake mix, oil, water, eggs and a few drops of red food coloring in a bowl and mix well. Stir in the pecans. Drop by rounded teaspoonfuls onto an ungreased cookie sheet. Top each cookie with a cherry quarter. Bake at 350 degrees for 10 to 12 minutes or until light brown. Cool on the cookie sheet for 1 minute. Remove to a wire rack to cool completely.

Makes 4 to 5 dozen cookies

Cherry Gingerbread Cookies

1 (15-ounce) package gingerbread
   cake mix

$^1/_2$ cup finely chopped dried cherries
1 cup coarse sugar

Prepare the cake mix using the package directions. Stir in the cherries. Shape into 1-inch balls. Place 2 inches apart on an ungreased cookie sheet. Lightly butter the bottom of a small glass and dip it in the sugar. Flatten the dough balls with the glass, dipping in additional sugar each time. Bake at 350 degrees for 12 to 14 minutes or until firm. Remove to a wire rack to cool completely.

Makes 2 dozen cookies

Easy Chocolate Cookies

1 (2-layer) package chocolate
   cake mix

$^1/_2$ cup (1 stick) butter, softened
2 eggs

Combine the cake mix, butter and eggs in a mixing bowl and beat until blended. Drop by spoonfuls onto a greased cookie sheet. Bake at 350 degrees for 15 minutes. Remove to a wire rack to cool completely. You may add chopped nuts, raisins, candy-coated chocolate candies, chocolate chips or mint chips to the dough if desired.

Makes 4 dozen cookies

**Store cooled crisp cookies in an airtight metal tin, and store
soft and chewy cookies in a plastic container.**

Chocolate Butterscotch Delights

1 (2-layer) package chocolate
  cake mix
2 eggs

$1/3$ cup vegetable oil
1 cup butterscotch chips

Combine the cake mix, eggs and oil in a large bowl and mix well. Add the butterscotch chips and mix well. Drop by rounded teaspoonfuls onto a greased cookie sheet. Bake at 350 degrees for 9 to 12 minutes or until golden brown. Remove to a wire rack to cool completely.

Makes 4 to 5 dozen cookies

Chocolate Chunk Cookies

1 (2-layer) package yellow cake mix
1 cup flour
$3/4$ cup ($1^1/2$ sticks) butter, melted
2 eggs

1 teaspoon vanilla extract
1 cup quick-cooking oatmeal
1 cup chopped walnuts
1 cup chocolate chips

Combine the cake mix, flour, butter, eggs and vanilla in a large mixing bowl and beat at low speed for 1 minute, scraping the side of the bowl. Beat at medium speed for 1 minute. Stir in the oatmeal, walnuts and chocolate chips. Drop by rounded teaspoonfuls 2 inches apart onto an ungreased cookie sheet.

Bake at 375 degrees for 12 to 15 minutes or until the edges are golden brown. Cool on the cookie sheet for 1 minute. Remove to a wire rack and let cool completely.

Makes 4 dozen cookies

Chocolate Cinnamon Chewies

1 (2-layer) package devil's food
   cake mix
1/3 cup water
1/4 cup (1/2 stick) butter, melted

1 egg
1 cup cinnamon chips
1/2 cup chopped walnuts

Combine the cake mix, water, butter and egg in a large mixing bowl and beat at low speed for 1 minute, scraping the side of the bowl. Beat at medium speed for 1 minute. Stir in the cinnamon chips and walnuts. Drop by teaspoonfuls onto a greased cookie sheet.

Bake at 350 degrees for 7 to 8 minutes or until firm. Cool on the cookie sheet for 3 minutes. Remove to a wire rack and let cool completely.

Makes 7 dozen cookies

Chocolate Sandwich Cookies

2 (2-layer) packages devil's food
   cake mix
4 eggs
1 1/2 cups shortening

8 ounces cream cheese, softened
1/2 cup (1 stick) margarine, softened
3 1/2 cups confectioners' sugar
1 teaspoon vanilla extract

Combine the cake mixes and eggs in a large bowl and mix well. Cut in the shortening until crumbly. Shape into balls. Place on an ungreased 12x18-inch cookie sheet. Bake at 350 degrees for 9 minutes or until the tops are cracked. Cool completely. Combine the cream cheese, margarine, confectioners' sugar and vanilla in a bowl and mix well. Spread between 2 cookies.

Makes 5 to 6 dozen cookies

Lemon Cookies

2 tablespoons fresh lemon juice
1 egg
1 (2-layer) package lemon cake mix

4 1/2 ounces whipped topping
1 cup confectioners' sugar

Combine the lemon juice and egg in a mixing bowl and blend well. Stir in the cake mix and whipped topping and beat until smooth and creamy. Chill for 8 hours. Shape with flour-coated hands into balls. Roll in the confectioners' sugar. Bake at 325 degrees for 8 minutes or until light brown. Remove to a wire rack to cool.

Makes 2 1/2 dozen cookies

Lemon Cranberry Biscotti

1 (2-layer) package white cake mix
1 cup flour
1/2 cup (1 stick) butter or margarine, melted
2 eggs
1 teaspoon vanilla extract

3/4 cup chopped dried sweetened cranberries
1/2 cup chopped nuts
2 tablespoons grated lemon zest
Semisweet chocolate chips, melted

Combine the cake mix, flour, butter, eggs and vanilla in a large bowl and beat at low speed until blended. Stir in the cranberries, nuts and lemon zest. Divide the dough in half. Shape each half into a 2x22-inch log. Place each log on a baking sheet lined with parchment paper. Bake each log separately at 350 degrees for 30 to 35 minutes or until a wooden pick inserted near the center comes out clean. Cool on the baking sheet for 15 minutes.

Cut each log into 1/2-inch slices on the diagonal. Arrange the slices on baking sheets. Bake at 350 degrees for 10 minutes. Remove to a wire rack and let cool completely. Dip 1 end of the biscotti in the melted chocolate. Let stand at room temperature until the chocolate is set.

Makes about 7 dozen cookies

Lemon Crispies

1 (2-layer) package lemon cake mix
1/2 cup (1 stick) butter

1 egg, beaten
1 cup crisp rice cereal

Combine the cake mix, butter and egg in a bowl and mix well. Add the cereal and mix well. Shape into 1 1/2-inch balls. Place on a baking sheet. Bake at 350 degrees for 8 to 10 minutes.

Makes 3 dozen cookies

Angel Macaroons

1 (16-ounce) package one-step angel food cake mix
1/2 cup sugar-free strawberry carbonated beverage
2 teaspoons vanilla or almond extract

2 cups unsweetened shredded coconut
1/2 cup chopped walnuts

Beat the cake mix, strawberry beverage and vanilla in a large mixing bowl at low speed for 30 seconds. Beat at medium speed for 1 minute, scraping the side of the bowl frequently. Fold in the coconut and walnuts. Drop by teaspoonfuls 2 inches apart onto a foil-lined cookie sheet. Bake at 350 degrees for 10 to 12 minutes or until brown. Let cool. Store in airtight containers.

Makes 5 dozen cookies

Sherbet Macaroons

2 cups sherbet, softened
1 (2-layer) package white cake mix

2 teaspoons almond extract
6 cups shredded coconut

Combine the sherbet, cake mix and almond extract in a mixing bowl and beat until blended. Stir in the coconut. Drop by tablespoonfuls 2 inches apart onto a buttered cookie sheet. Bake at 350 degrees for 12 to 15 minutes or until the edges are golden brown.

Makes 5 to 6 dozen cookies

Orange Crinkles

1 (2-layer) package orange cake mix
1/2 cup vegetable oil

2 eggs
1 tablespoon grated orange zest

Combine the cake mix, oil, eggs and grated orange zest in a medium bowl and mix well. Drop by spoonfuls onto an ungreased baking sheet. Bake at 350 degrees for 10 minutes or until light brown. Cool on the baking sheet for 1 minute. Remove to a wire rack to cool completely. You may top each slice with a pecan half before baking.

Makes 3 dozen cookies

Orange Slice Cookies

1 (1-layer) package yellow cake mix
1 egg
3 tablespoons vegetable oil

1 cup chopped pecans
10 orange slice candies, chopped
1/2 cup chopped dates (optional)

Combine the cake mix, egg and oil in a bowl and mix well. Stir in the pecans, candies and dates. Drop by spoonfuls 2 inches apart onto an ungreased cookie sheet. Bake at 350 degrees for 8 to 10 minutes or until the edges begin to brown. Remove to a wire rack to cool.

Makes 2$^1/_2$ dozen cookies

Peanut Butter Cookies

1 (2-layer) package yellow cake mix
1 cup peanut butter
1/2 cup vegetable oil

2 tablespoons water
2 eggs

Combine the cake mix, peanut butter, oil, water and eggs in a bowl and mix well. Drop by teaspoonfuls 2 inches apart onto an ungreased cookie sheet. Dip a fork in water. Press crisscross on each cookie. Bake at 350 degrees for 10 to 12 minutes. Cool on the cookie sheet for 1 minute. Remove to a wire rack to cool completely.

Makes 2 dozen cookies

Pumpkin Spice Cookies

1 (2-layer) package spice cake mix   1 (15-ounce) can pumpkin

Combine the cake mix and pumpkin in a bowl and mix well. Drop by rounded teaspoonfuls onto a greased cookie sheet. Bake at 350 degrees for 8 to 10 minutes or until golden brown. Cool on the cookie sheet for 5 minutes. Remove to a wire rack to cool completely.

Makes 2 dozen cookies

Raisin-Cream Cheese Cookies

1/4 cup (1/2 stick) butter, softened   1 (2-layer) package yellow cake mix
8 ounces cream cheese, softened   1 1/4 cups raisins
1 egg yolk   1/4 cup shredded coconut
1 teaspoon vanilla extract   1/4 cup chopped walnuts

Cream the butter, cream cheese, egg yolk and vanilla in a mixing bowl. Blend in the cake mix 1/3 at a time, mixing the last portion by hand. Stir in the raisins, coconut and walnuts. Drop by level tablespoonfuls 2 inches apart onto a greased cookie sheet. Bake at 350 degrees for 15 minutes or until light brown. Cool on a wire rack. You may substitute margarine for the butter and white cake mix for the yellow cake mix.

Makes 4 dozen cookies

**Don't let cookies cool on the cookie sheet for more than
1 minute after they have been removed from the oven. They will
continue to cook on the hot surface and will become hard
to remove from the cookie sheet.**

Raisin-Spice Cookies

1 (2-layer) package spice cake mix
1 cup quick-cooking oatmeal
1/2 cup (1 stick) butter, softened

2 eggs
1/2 cup raisins
Cinnamon to taste

Combine the cake mix, oatmeal, butter and eggs in a mixing bowl. Beat at low speed until mixed, scraping the bowl occasionally. Stir in the raisins. Drop by rounded teaspoonfuls onto a greased cookie sheet. Bake at 350 degrees for 7 to 9 minutes or until light brown. Sprinkle with cinnamon. Remove to a wire rack to cool.

Makes 4 dozen cookies

Strawberry Cookies

1 (2-layer) package strawberry
  cake mix
2 eggs, beaten

1/2 cup chopped fresh strawberries
1 cup whipping cream, whipped

Combine the cake mix, eggs and strawberries in a bowl and mix well. Fold in the whipped cream. Drop by rounded teaspoonfuls onto a greased cookie sheet.

Bake at 350 degrees for 8 to 10 minutes or until golden brown. Cool on the cookie sheet for 5 minutes. Remove to a wire rack to cool completely.

Makes 2 1/2 dozen cookies

Cake Mix Cookies

1 (2-layer) package any flavor
   cake mix
1 egg, beaten

8 ounces whipped topping
2 cups sifted confectioners' sugar

Combine the cake mix and egg in a mixing bowl and beat well. Add the whipped topping and mix well. Shape into balls. The mixture will be sticky. Roll in the confectioners' sugar to coat. Place on a cookie sheet. Bake at 350 degrees for 8 to 10 minutes or until the cookies are set. Cool on the cookie sheet for several minutes. Remove to a wire rack to cool completely.

Makes 3 dozen cookies

Snowflake Cookies

1 (2-layer) package white cake mix
1 cup (2 sticks) butter or margarine,
   softened

1 egg
1 teaspoon vanilla extract
2 cups quick-cooking oatmeal

Combine half the cake mix, the butter, egg and vanilla in a large bowl and mix well with a wooden spoon. Stir in the remaining cake mix and oatmeal. Divide the dough in half. Roll each half 1/4 inch thick on a floured surface. Cut with a 3-inch snowflake cookie cutter. Place on an ungreased cookie sheet.

Bake at 350 degrees for 6 to 8 minutes or until the edges are set. The centers may still be soft. Remove to a wire rack to cool completely. You may decorate with colored sugar, candy sprinkles or icing if desired.

Makes 2 to 3 dozen cookies

Snickerdoodles

1 (2-layer) yellow cake mix
2 eggs
1/4 cup vegetable oil

3 tablespoons sugar
1 teaspoon cinnamon

Combine the cake mix, eggs and oil in a large bowl and stir until blended. Shape the dough into 1-inch balls. Roll in a mixture of the sugar and cinnamon. Place 2 inches apart on a greased cookie sheet. Flatten the balls with the bottom of a glass. Bake at 375 degrees for 8 to 9 minutes or until set. Cool on the cookie sheet for 1 minute. Remove to a wire rack to cool completely.

Makes 3 dozen cookies

Quick-as-a-Wink Sugar Cookies

1 (2-layer) package yellow cake mix
1/2 cup vegetable oil
2 tablespoons water

2 eggs, beaten
Sugar

Combine the cake mix, oil, water and eggs in a bowl and mix well. Drop by teaspoonfuls onto an ungreased cookie sheet. Dip a wet glass bottom in sugar. Flatten the cookies with the glass. Bake at 350 degrees for 10 to 12 minutes. Cool on the cookie sheet for 1 minute. Remove to a wire rack to cool completely.

Makes 4 to 5 dozen cookies

Apple Squares

3/4 cup (1 1/2 sticks) margarine,
   softened
1 (2-layer) package white cake mix

1 (21-ounce) can apple pie filling
1/2 cup flaked coconut

Cut the margarine into the cake mix in a bowl until crumbly. Reserve 1 cup of the crumb mixture. Press the remaining mixture into a 9x13-inch baking pan. Spoon the pie filling evenly over the crumb mixture. Sprinkle with a mixture of the reserved crumbs and coconut. Bake at 350 degrees for 45 minutes or until golden brown. Cool slightly. Cut into squares.

Serves 24

Apricot Preserve Bars

1 (2-layer) package yellow cake mix
1/3 cup margarine or butter, softened
1 egg
1/2 cup apricot preserves
1 cup sugar
3 eggs

2 tablespoons margarine, softened
2 tablespoons flour
1/4 teaspoon baking powder
Salt to taste
1 1/2 cups flaked coconut

Combine the cake mix, 1/3 cup margarine and 1 egg in a bowl and mix well. Press into a greased 10x15-inch baking pan. Bake at 350 degrees for 10 to 12 minutes or until light brown. The crust will be soft. Cool slightly in the pan. Spread the preserves over the crust. Cream the sugar, 3 eggs and 2 tablespoons margarine in a mixing bowl until light and fluffy. Add the flour, baking powder and salt and mix well. Stir in the coconut. Spread evenly over the preserves. Bake for 15 to 20 minutes or until light brown. Cool in the pan. Cut into bars. You may substitute strawberry preserves for the apricot preserves if preferred.

Makes 3 to 4 dozen bars

Caramel Layer Squares

1 (14-ounce) package light caramels
1/3 cup evaporated milk
1 (2-layer) package German
   chocolate cake mix with pudding

3/4 cup (11/2 sticks) butter or
   margarine, melted
1/3 cup evaporated milk
1 cup semisweet chocolate chips

Combine the caramels and 1/3 cup evaporated milk in a heavy saucepan. Cook over low heat until the caramels are melted, stirring constantly. Keep warm. Combine the cake mix, butter and 1/3 cup evaporated milk in a large bowl. Mix until a soft dough forms. Press half the dough into a greased 9x13-inch baking pan. Bake at 350 degrees for 10 minutes. Sprinkle the chocolate chips over the crust. Spread with the caramel mixture. Crumble the reserved dough over the top. Bake for 25 to 30 minutes or until the topping is brown.

Serves 36

Caramel Pecan Dream Bars

1 (2-layer) package yellow cake mix
1/3 cup margarine, softened
1 egg
1 (14-ounce) can sweetened
   condensed milk

1 egg
1 teaspoon vanilla extract
1 cup chopped pecans
1/2 cup Heath Bits 'O Brickle
   baking chips

Combine the cake mix, margarine and 1 egg in a large mixing bowl and beat at high speed until crumbly. Press into a greased 9x13-inch baking pan. Combine the condensed milk, 1 egg and vanilla in a small mixing bowl and beat until blended. Stir in the pecans and baking chips. Pour over the batter. Bake at 350 degrees for 25 to 35 minutes or until the center is light golden brown. Cool completely. Cut into bars.

Makes 2 dozen bars

Cheesecake Bars

1/2 cup (1 stick) margarine, softened
1 egg
1 (2-layer) package yellow cake mix
8 ounces cream cheese, softened

2 eggs
1 (1-pound) package confectioners' sugar

Combine the margarine, 1 egg and cake mix in a bowl and mix well. Pat into a greased 10x13-inch baking pan. Beat the cream cheese in a mixing bowl until smooth. Beat in 2 eggs until blended. Add the confectioners' sugar and mix well. Spoon over the mixture in the prepared pan. Bake at 350 degrees for 45 minutes or until golden brown. Let stand until cool. Cut into bars.

Serves 28

Cherry Cobbler Bars

1 (2-layer) package yellow cake mix
1/4 cup (1/2 stick) butter, softened
2 eggs
1 (21-ounce) can cherry pie filling

1 (7-ounce) package coconut-pecan frosting mix
2 tablespoons butter, melted

Grease the bottom of a 9x13-inch baking pan. Combine the cake mix, 1/4 cup butter and eggs in a large bowl and mix well. Press into the prepared pan. Pour the pie filling over the prepared layer. Combine the frosting mix and 2 tablespoons butter in a bowl and mix well. Sprinkle over the cherry layer. Bake at 350 degrees for 30 minutes. Let stand until cool. Cut into bars.

Serves 12 to 16

Black Forest Squares

1 (2-layer) package chocolate
  cake mix
1 (21-ounce) can cherry pie filling
2 eggs, beaten

2¹/2 cups confectioners' sugar
¹/2 cup baking cocoa
¹/2 cup (1 stick) margarine
¹/4 cup water

Combine the cake mix, pie filling and eggs in a bowl and mix well. Spoon into a greased 11x17-inch baking pan. Bake at 350 degrees for 35 minutes. Cool completely. Sift the confectioners' sugar and baking cocoa into a bowl. Combine the margarine and water in a microwave-safe bowl. Microwave on High for 30 seconds. Add the cocoa mixture and mix well. Spread over the cake. Cut into squares.

Serves 12 to 16

Double Chocolate Layer Bars

1 (2-layer) package German
  chocolate cake mix
1 egg
¹/2 cup (1 stick) margarine, melted
2 cups flaked coconut

3/4 cup milk chocolate chips
3/4 cup butterscotch chips
¹/2 cup chopped pecans
1 (14-ounce) can sweetened
  condensed milk

Combine the cake mix, egg and margarine in a bowl and mix well. Press firmly into a 9x13-inch baking pan. Sprinkle with the coconut, chocolate chips, butterscotch chips and pecans. Spread the condensed milk evenly over the top to the edges of the pan. Bake at 350 degrees for 30 minutes. Cool completely. Cut into bars.

Serves 20 to 24

Chocolate Peanut Butter Bars

1 (2-layer) package devil's food
   cake mix
1/2 cup (1 stick) margarine, melted

3/4 cup creamy peanut butter
1 (8-ounce) jar marshmallow crème

Combine the cake mix and margarine in a bowl and mix well. Reserve 1 cup of the cake mixture. Press the remaining mixture in a greased 9x13-inch baking pan. Combine the peanut butter and marshmallow crème in a bowl and mix well. Spread the peanut butter mixture evenly over the cake mix layer. Sprinkle the reserved cake mixture over the top. Bake at 350 degrees for 20 minutes. Let stand until cool. Cut into bars.

Serves 12 to 16

Fudge-Filled Peanut Butter Bars

1 (2-layer) package yellow cake mix
1 cup peanut butter
1/2 cup (1 stick) margarine, melted
2 eggs
1 1/3 cups sweetened condensed milk
2 cups milk chocolate chips

2 tablespoons margarine
1/2 teaspoon salt
2 teaspoons vanilla extract
1 cup flaked coconut (optional)
1 cup chopped nuts (optional)

Combine the cake mix, peanut butter, 1/2 cup margarine and eggs in a mixing bowl and mix well. Press 2/3 of the mixture into a 9x13-inch baking pan. Combine the condensed milk, chocolate chips, 2 tablespoons margarine and salt in a heavy saucepan. Cook until smooth, stirring frequently. Remove from the heat. Stir in the vanilla, coconut and nuts. Spread in the prepared pan. Top with the remaining cake mixture. Bake at 350 degrees for 20 minutes. Cool on a wire rack. Cut into bars.

Makes 3 dozen bars

Peanut Cream Chocolate Bars

1 (2-layer) package devil's food
  cake mix
1/3 cup corn oil
1 egg
1/2 cup sugar

3/4 cup peanut butter
8 ounces cream cheese, softened
1 egg
1 teaspoon vanilla extract

Combine the cake mix, oil and 1 egg in a bowl and mix well. Reserve 1 cup for the topping. Press the remaining mixture into a 9x13-inch baking pan. Bake at 350 degrees for 10 minutes. Cool completely. Combine the sugar, peanut butter, cream cheese, 1 egg and vanilla in a bowl and mix well. Spread over the baked layer. Sprinkle the reserved cake mixture over the top. Bake at 350 degrees for 20 minutes. Chill for 1 hour. Cut into bars.

Serves 24

Gooey Coconut Bars

1 (2-layer) package French vanilla
  cake mix
2 eggs
1/2 cup (1 stick) butter or margarine,
  melted
8 ounces cream cheese, softened

2 eggs
1 teaspoon vanilla extract
1/2 teaspoon almond extract
1 (1-pound) package confectioners'
  sugar
1 1/2 cups shredded coconut

Combine the cake mix, 2 eggs and butter in a bowl and mix well. Press the mixture over the bottom and 1 inch up the side of a 9x13-inch baking pan sprayed with nonstick cooking spray. Combine the cream cheese, 2 eggs, flavorings, confectioners' sugar and coconut in a bowl and mix well. Spread the mixture evenly over the prepared layer. Bake at 350 degrees for 45 minutes or until golden brown on top. Let stand until cool. Cut into bars.

Serves 16

Coconut Pecan Bars

1 (2-layer) package spice cake mix
1/2 cup (1 stick) butter, softened
1 egg
1/4 cup milk
1 1/2 cups sugar
1 (12-ounce) can evaporated milk

3/4 cup (1 1/2 sticks) butter, chopped
5 egg yolks
3 cups sweetened flaked coconut
1 1/2 cups chopped pecans
1 teaspoon cinnamon
1/4 teaspoon ground cloves

Combine the cake mix, 1/2 cup butter, 1 egg and milk in a bowl and beat for 2 minutes or until smooth. Spread the mixture in a 10x15-inch baking pan sprayed with nonstick cooking spray. Bake at 350 degrees for 18 to 20 minutes or until a wooden pick inserted in the center comes out clean. Let stand until cool.

Combine the sugar, evaporated milk, 3/4 cup butter and egg yolks in a medium saucepan. Simmer over medium heat for 1 minute or until thickened, stirring constantly. Remove from the heat and stir in the coconut, pecans, cinnamon and cloves. Frost the baked layer. Let stand for 2 hours or until cool. Cut into bars.

Serves 36

Lemon Angel Bars

1 (16-ounce) package one-step angel
    food cake mix
1 (21-ounce) can lemon pie filling

1/3 cup margarine, softened
2 cups confectioners' sugar
1 tablespoon lemon juice

Combine the cake mix and pie filling in a bowl and mix well. Pour into a greased 12x18-inch baking pan. Bake at 350 degrees for 15 minutes or until firm. Combine the margarine, confectioners' sugar and lemon juice in a mixing bowl and mix well. Spread over the baked layer. Cut into bars.

Serves 24

Lemon Chess Bars

1 (2-layer) package lemon cake mix
1/2 cup (1 stick) butter or margarine, melted
3 eggs

8 ounces cream cheese, softened
1 (1-pound) package confectioners' sugar

Combine the cake mix, butter and 1 of the eggs in a mixing bowl and beat well. Press over the bottom of a greased 9x13-inch baking pan. Combine the remaining 2 eggs, cream cheese and confectioners' sugar in a mixing bowl and beat well. Pour into the prepared pan. Bake at 325 degrees for 55 minutes. Cool slightly. Cut into bars. If using a glass baking dish, bake for 40 to 45 minutes or until light brown.

Serves 15

Peach Crisp Bars

1 (16-ounce) can peaches
1 (2-layer) package butter-pecan cake mix

1 cup flaked coconut
1 cup chopped pecans

Chop the peaches. Spread the peaches with juice in a 9x13-inch nonstick baking pan. Sprinkle with the cake mix, coconut and pecans. Bake at 350 degrees for 35 to 40 minutes or until golden brown. Cool completely.

Serves 24

Salted Nut Bars

1 (2-layer) package yellow cake mix
2/3 cup margarine
1 egg
3 cups miniature marshmallows
2/3 cup light corn syrup

2 cups peanut butter chips
1/4 cup (1/2 stick) margarine
2 teaspoons vanilla extract
2 cups crisp rice cereal
2 cups salted peanuts

Combine the cake mix, 2/3 cup margarine and egg in a mixing bowl. Beat at low speed until well mixed. Press into a greased 9x13-inch baking pan. Bake at 350 degrees for 12 to 18 minutes. Sprinkle the marshmallows over the top. Bake for 1 to 2 minutes or until the marshmallows begin to puff. Cool completely. Heat the corn syrup, peanut butter chips, 1/4 cup margarine and vanilla in a saucepan over low heat until blended, stirring constantly. Remove from the heat. Stir in the cereal and peanuts. Spoon over the marshmallow layer. Cut into bars. Store, covered, in the refrigerator.

Serves 24

Butter Pecan Bars

1 (2-layer) package butter-pecan
  cake mix
1 egg
1/2 cup (1 stick) butter or margarine,
  melted
3 1/2 cups confectioners' sugar

8 ounces cream cheese, softened
1/2 cup (1 stick) butter or margarine,
  melted
2 eggs
1/4 to 1/2 cup chopped pecans

Combine the cake mix, 1 egg and 1/2 cup butter in a bowl and mix until crumbly. Press into a buttered 9x13inch baking pan. Combine the confectioners' sugar, cream cheese, 1/2 cup butter and 2 eggs in a bowl and mix well. Pour evenly over the prepared layer. Sprinkle with the pecans. Bake at 350 degrees for 55 minutes. Let stand until cool. Cut into bars.

Serves 12 to 16

Pecan Cream Cheese Bars

1 (2-layer) package yellow cake mix
3/4 cup chopped pecans
3/4 cup (1 1/2 sticks) margarine, melted

16 ounces cream cheese, softened
1 cup packed brown sugar
3/4 cup chopped pecans

Combine the cake mix and 3/4 cup pecans in a bowl and mix well. Add the margarine and mix well. Press evenly over the bottom of a 9x13-inch baking pan. Combine the cream cheese and brown sugar in a mixing bowl and beat until blended. Spread evenly over the cake mix layer. Sprinkle with 3/4 cup pecans. Bake at 350 degrees for 25 to 30 minutes or until the edges are brown and the cream cheese mixture is set. Cool in the pan on a wire rack. Cut into bars. Store, covered, in the refrigerator.

Serves 24

Pumpkin Cheesecake Bars

1 (16-ounce) package pound cake mix
1 egg
2 tablespoons margarine, melted
2 teaspoons pumpkin pie spice
8 ounces cream cheese, softened
1 (14-ounce) can sweetened
   condensed milk

2 eggs
1 (16-ounce) can pumpkin
2 teaspoons pumpkin pie spice
1/2 teaspoon salt
1 cup chopped nuts

Combine the cake mix, 1 egg, margarine and 2 teaspoons pumpkin pie spice in a mixing bowl. Beat at low speed until crumbly. Press over the bottom of a 10x15-inch baking pan. Beat the cream cheese in a mixing bowl at high speed until fluffy. Beat in the condensed milk gradually. Add 2 eggs, the pumpkin, 2 teaspoons pumpkin pie spice and salt and mix well. Spoon over the prepared crust. Sprinkle with the nuts. Bake at 350 degrees for 30 to 35 minutes or until set. Let stand until cool. Chill, covered, until serving time. Cut into bars. Store, covered, in the refrigerator.

Serves 36

Raspberry Bars

1 (2-layer) package yellow cake mix
1¹/₂ cups quick-cooking oatmeal
³/₄ cup (1¹/₂ sticks) butter, melted

1 (12-ounce) jar raspberry jam
1 tablespoon water

Combine the cake mix and oatmeal in a bowl and mix well. Add the butter and mix until crumbly. Press 3 cups of the mixture into a 9x13-inch baking pan. Combine the jam and water in a small bowl and mix well. Spread evenly over the prepared layer. Sprinkle with the remaining crumb mixture. Bake at 375 degrees for 25 minutes. Let stand until cool. Cut into bars.

Serves 10 to 12

Butterscotch Brownie Bars

¹/₂ cup vegetable oil
2 tablespoons water
2 eggs
1 (2-layer) package yellow cake mix

2 cups miniature marshmallows
1 cup butterscotch, peanut butter or
    chocolate chips

Combine the oil, water and eggs in a small bowl and mix well. Add to the cake mix in a large bowl and mix well. Stir in the marshmallows and butterscotch chips. Spread in a 9x13-inch baking pan sprayed with nonstick cooking spray. Bake at 325 degrees for 40 to 45 minutes or until the brownies spring back when lightly touched. Let cool. Cut into 2-inch bars.

Serves 15 to 20

Brownies

1 (2-layer) package German
  chocolate cake mix
1 cup chopped pecans
1/3 cup evaporated milk
3/4 cup (1 1/2 sticks) butter, melted

1 (14-ounce) package vanilla
  caramels
1/2 cup evaporated milk
1 cup semisweet chocolate chips

Combine the cake mix, pecans, 1/3 cup evaporated milk and butter in a bowl and mix well. Press half the mixture into a greased 9x13-inch baking dish. Bake at 350 degrees for 8 minutes. Heat the caramels and 1/2 cup evaporated milk in a double boiler until the caramels melt, stirring occasionally. Pour over the baked layer. Top with the chocolate chips. Top with the remaining pecan mixture. Bake at 350 degrees for 18 minutes. Let cool. Cut into squares.

Serves 15

Majestic Brownies

1 (2-layer) package chocolate cake
  mix
1/3 cup vegetable oil
1 egg
1 (14-ounce) can sweetened
  condensed milk

1 cup semisweet chocolate chips
1 cup chopped pecans
1 teaspoon vanilla extract
Dash of salt

Combine the cake mix, oil and egg in a blender and process until crumbly. Press half the mixture into a greased 9x13-inch baking pan. Combine the condensed milk, chocolate chips, pecans, vanilla and salt in bowl and mix well. Spread in the prepared pan. Top with the remaining crumbly mixture. Bake at 350 degrees for 30 to 45 minutes or until the brownies test done. Cool completely. Cut into squares.

Serves 12 to 15

Triple-Threat Chocolate Brownies

1 (4-ounce) package chocolate
  pudding mix
2 cups milk
1 (2-layer) package chocolate
  cake mix

1 cup milk chocolate chips
1/2 cup chopped pecans (optional)
Whipped topping

Prepare the pudding mix with the milk using the package directions for microwave preparation. Cool slightly. Fold the pudding into the cake mix in a bowl. Add the chocolate chips and pecans and stir gently. Pour into a lightly greased and floured 9x12-inch baking pan. Bake at 350 degrees for 30 minutes or until a wooden pick inserted near the center comes out clean. Let cool. Cut into squares. Top each serving with a dollop of whipped topping.

Serves 12 to 20

The Ultimate Brownie

1 (2-layer) package chocolate
  cake mix
1 egg, beaten
1/2 cup (1 stick) butter
1 cup chopped pecans or walnuts

1 tablespoon water
8 ounces cream cheese, softened
3 eggs
1 (1-pound) package confectioners'
  sugar

Combine the cake mix, 1 egg, butter, pecans and water in a bowl and mix well. Press into a greased 9x13-inch baking pan. Combine the cream cheese, 3 eggs and confectioners' sugar in a mixing bowl and mix until smooth. Pour over the chocolate layer. Bake at 350 to 375 degrees for 30 to 45 minutes or until golden brown. You may substitute lemon or yellow cake mix for chocolate if preferred.

Serves 12 to 16

Just Desserts

Frozen Angel Food Fruit Dessert

1 (16-ounce) package angel food
  cake mix
1/2 gallon vanilla ice cream, softened
1 (11-ounce) can mandarin oranges,
  drained
1 (3-ounce) package orange gelatin

1 cup blueberries
1 (3-ounce) package lime gelatin
1 1/2 cups sliced strawberries
1 (3-ounce) package strawberry
  gelatin

Prepare and bake the cake mix using the package directions. Invert onto a funnel to cool completely. Remove the cake from the pan and tear into small pieces. Press 1/4 of the cake pieces in the bottom of a 10-inch tube pan. Layer 1/4 of the ice cream and the mandarin oranges over the cake layer. Sprinkle evenly with the orange gelatin mix. Layer 1/4 of the cake pieces, 1/4 of the ice cream and the blueberries over the orange gelatin layer. Sprinkle evenly with the lime gelatin mix. Layer 1/4 of the cake pieces, 1/4 of the ice cream and the strawberries over the lime gelatin layer. Sprinkle evenly with the strawberry gelatin mix. Layer the remaining cake pieces and remaining ice cream over the top. Freeze, covered, until ready to serve. Invert onto a serving plate and cut into slices.

Serves 12

Apricot Nectar Delight

1 (16-ounce) package angel food
  cake mix
1 (46-ounce) can apricot nectar
1 1/2 cups sugar

7 rounded tablespoons cornstarch
8 ounces whipped topping
Chopped walnuts

Prepare and bake the cake mix using the package directions. Invert onto a funnel to cool completely. Remove the cake from the pan and tear into small pieces. Arrange the cake pieces in a 9x13-inch pan. Cook a mixture of the next 3 ingredients over medium heat until thickened, stirring constantly. Remove from the heat and let cool slightly. Pour over the cake and chill, covered. Spread the whipped topping over the top and sprinkle with walnuts.

Serves 12

Blueberry Dessert

1 (16-ounce) package angel food
    cake mix
8 ounces cream cheese, softened
1 cup confectioners' sugar

8 ounces whipped topping
$1^1/_2$ teaspoons grated orange zest
2 (2-ounce) cans blueberry pie filling

Prepare and bake the cake mix using the package directions. Invert onto a funnel to cool completely. Remove the cake from the pan and tear into small pieces. Combine the cream cheese and confectioners' sugar in a mixing bowl and beat until smooth. Fold in the whipped topping and orange zest. Add the cake pieces and mix well. Spread the mixture in a 9x13-inch pan. Spread the pie filling evenly over the top. Chill, covered, for 2 hours.

Serves 15

Banana Split Cake

1 (16-ounce) package angel food
    cake mix
1 (21-ounce) can cherry pie filling
1 (20-ounce) can crushed pineapple
2 (4-ounce) packages vanilla instant
    pudding mix, prepared

3 or 4 bananas, sliced into
    $1/_4$-inch pieces
16 ounces whipped topping

Prepare and bake the cake mix using the package directions. Invert onto a funnel to cool completely. Remove the cake from the pan and tear into small pieces. Layer the cake pieces, pie filling, undrained pineapple, pudding, bananas and whipped topping $1/_2$ at a time in a large serving bowl. You may use light pie filling, pineapple in its own juice, sugar-free pudding and light whipped topping for a lower-calorie dessert.

Serves 20 to 30

Raspberry Rhapsody

1 (16-ounce) package angel food
  cake mix
1 (3-ounce) package strawberry
  gelatin
1 1/2 cups hot water
1 (10-ounce) package frozen
  raspberries, thawed

2 cups whipping cream
1/2 cup sugar
2 teaspoons vanilla extract
1 tablespoon sugar
1 tablespoon cornstarch

Prepare and bake the cake mix using the package directions. Invert onto a funnel to cool completely. Remove the cake from the pan. Remove the crust from the cake and tear into small pieces. Combine the gelatin and hot water in a bowl and mix well. Chill until slightly thickened.

Drain the raspberries, reserving the juice. Beat the whipping cream in a mixing bowl until soft peaks form. Add 1/2 cup sugar and the vanilla, beating until stiff peaks form. Whip the gelatin with 1 tablespoon sugar for 5 minutes. Fold the gelatin mixture into the whipped cream. Stir in the raspberries.

Layer the gelatin mixture and angel food cake alternately in a tube pan until all the ingredients are used, beginning and ending with the gelatin mixture. Chill, covered, overnight. Invert onto a serving platter. Combine the reserved raspberry juice and cornstarch in a saucepan and mix well. Cook until thickened, stirring constantly. Drizzle over the top.

Serves 16

Pumpkin Trifle

1 (2-layer) spice cake mix
4 (4-ounce) packages butterscotch
    instant pudding mix
2$1/2$ cups milk
1 teaspoon cinnamon

$1/4$ teaspoon nutmeg
$1/4$ teaspoon ground ginger
$1/4$ teaspoon allspice
1 (29-ounce) can pumpkin
2 cups whipping cream, whipped

Prepare and bake the cake mix using the package directions. Let cool completely. Crumble half the cake into a trifle bowl. Prepare the pudding according to the package directions, using 2$1/2$ cups milk. Blend the cinnamon, nutmeg, ginger and allspice into the pumpkin in a bowl. Mix the pudding and pumpkin mixture together in a bowl. Layer half the pudding mixture and half the whipped cream over the spice cake crumbs. Crumble $3/4$ of the remaining spice cake over the whipped cream. Repeat the pudding mixture and whipped cream layers. Crumble the remaining spice cake over the top.

Serves more than 25

Strawberry Angel Trifle

1 (16-ounce) package angel food
    cake mix
2 (3-ounce) packages strawberry
    gelatin
2$1/2$ cups boiling water

1 (16-ounce) package frozen
    strawberries
1 tablespoon sugar
$1/8$ teaspoon salt
2 envelopes dry whipped topping mix

Prepare and bake the cake mix using the package directions. Invert onto a funnel to cool completely. Remove the cake from the pan and tear into pieces. Dissolve the gelatin in the boiling water in a bowl. Stir in the frozen strawberries until thawed. Add the sugar and salt and mix well. Chill until thickened. Prepare the whipped topping using the package directions. Stir half the whipped topping into the strawberry mixture. Layer the cake pieces and strawberry mixture in a bundt pan. Chill until firm. Invert onto a serving plate. Spread the remaining whipped topping over the top and side.

Serves 24

Strawberry Raspberry Chocolate Trifle

1 (2-layer) package devil's food or
  German chocolate cake mix
1 (14-ounce) can sweetened
  condensed milk
1 cup cold water
1 (4-serving) package vanilla instant
  pudding mix

2 cups whipping cream, whipped
  until stiff peaks form
2 tablespoons orange juice
2 cups fresh strawberries, sliced
2 cups fresh raspberries
2 cups sliced peeled kiwifruit
  (optional)

Prepare the cake mix using the package directions. Pour into a greased 10x15-inch cake pan. Bake at 350 degrees for 20 minutes or until a wooden pick inserted in the center comes out clean. Remove to a wire rack to cool completely. Crumble enough of the cake to make 8 cups; reserve the remaining cake for another use. Combine the condensed milk and water in a mixing bowl and beat until smooth. Add the pudding mix and beat at low speed for 2 minutes or until slightly thickened. Fold in the whipped cream. Spread 2 1/2 cups of the pudding mixture in a 4-quart glass bowl. Layer half the cake crumbs over the pudding mixture. Sprinkle with half the orange juice, and layer half the strawberries, half the raspberries and half the kiwifruit over the cake layer. Repeat the pudding and cake layers and sprinkle with the remaining orange juice. Spread the remaining pudding mixture over the cake layer and spoon the remaining fruit over the top. Chill, covered, until serving time.

Serves 12 to 16

Angel Fruit Trifle

1 (16-ounce) package angel food
    cake mix
1 (11-ounce) can mandarin oranges,
    drained
1 (16-ounce) can sliced peaches,
    drained and chopped
1 (21-ounce) can cherry pie filling
2 bananas, sliced

1 (16-ounce) can prepared vanilla
    pudding
1 quart fresh strawberries or
    1 (16-ounce) package frozen
    raspberries or blueberries
1/2 cup sugar
8 ounces whipped topping

Prepare and bake the cake mix using the package directions. Invert onto a funnel to cool completely. Remove the cake from the pan and tear into small pieces. Layer 1/3 of the cake pieces, half the mandarin oranges, half the peaches and all the pie filling, then half the remaining cake pieces, the remaining mandarin oranges and peaches, the bananas and vanilla pudding and remaining cake pieces in a large trifle bowl.

Reserve several whole strawberries. Crush the remaining strawberries with the sugar in a bowl. Spoon the strawberry mixture over the cake pieces. Spread the whipped topping over the layers. Chill, covered, for 3 hours. Garnish with the reserved whole strawberries just before serving.

Serves 16 to 24

Chocolate Parfait Dessert

1 (2-layer) package devil's food
  cake mix
1/2 cup (1 stick) margarine, melted
1/4 cup milk
1 egg
3/4 cup finely chopped peanuts
3/4 cup peanut butter
1 1/2 cups confectioners' sugar
8 ounces cream cheese, softened

2 1/2 cups milk
8 ounces frozen whipped topping,
  thawed
1 (5-ounce) package vanilla instant
  pudding mix
1/2 cup chopped peanuts
1 (1 1/2-ounce) bar milk chocolate,
  chilled and grated

Grease and flour the bottom of a 9x13-inch baking pan. Combine the cake mix, margarine, 1/4 cup milk, egg and 3/4 cup peanuts in a mixing bowl and beat at medium speed until blended. Spread evenly into the prepared baking pan. Bake at 350 degrees for 20 to 25 minutes or until the cake tests done. Do not overbake. Let cool completely.

Combine the peanut butter and confectioners' sugar in a mixing bowl and beat at low speed until crumbly. Beat the cream cheese in large mixing bowl until smooth. Add 2 1/2 cups milk, the whipped topping and pudding mix and beat at low speed for 2 minutes or until blended.

Pour half the cream cheese mixture over the baked layer. Sprinkle with half the peanut butter mixture. Repeat with the remaining cream cheese and peanut butter mixtures. Sprinkle with 1/2 cup peanuts; gently press into filling. Sprinkle with the grated chocolate. Refrigerate or freeze, covered, until ready to serve.

Serves 12

Filled Chocolate Cupcakes

1 (2-layer) package chocolate cake mix	1/3 cup sugar
8 ounces cream cheese, softened	1 egg
	1 cup semisweet chocolate chips

Prepare the cake mix using the package directions. Fill paper-lined muffin cups 2/3 full with the mixture. Beat the cream cheese and sugar in a mixing bowl until light and fluffy. Beat in the egg. Stir in the chocolate chips. Drop 1 rounded teaspoon of the cream cheese mixture into each cupcake. Bake using the package directions for muffins.

Serves 30

Ice Cream Cone Cupcakes

Prepare your favorite flavored cake mix using the package directions. Place flat-bottomed cones in muffin cups. Fill 2/3 full with the prepared cake mix. Bake at 350 degrees for 15 to 20 minutes. Cool, frost and decorate as desired.

Serves variable

If you want to make a cheesecake but your cream cheese is not at room temperature, warm it quickly in the microwave oven. Unwrap the cream cheese, place it on a microwave-safe plate, and microwave on High for 20 to 30 seconds.

Sweet Orange Nuggets

Orange Nuggets

1 (2-layer) package orange cake mix
3 eggs
1/3 cup vegetable oil

1 cup orange juice
1 (11-ounce) can mandarin oranges,
   drained and chopped

Orange Glaze

2 cups confectioners' sugar

1 cup orange juice

For the nuggets, combine the cake mix, eggs, oil and orange juice in a large mixing bowl and mix well. Fold in the oranges. Pour into small paper-lined muffin cups. Bake at 350 degrees for 10 to 15 minutes or until the nuggets test done. Cool on a wire rack. Remove from the pans.

For the glaze, mix the confectioners' sugar and orange juice in a saucepan. Bring to a boil, stirring constantly. Remove from the heat and let cool. Dip the nuggets into the glaze.

Makes 50 nuggets

Ice Cream Sandwiches

1 (2-layer) package devil's food
   cake mix
1/2 cup shortening
1/4 cup (1/2 stick) butter, softened

1 egg
1 teaspoon vanilla extract
Your favorite flavor ice cream

Combine half the cake mix, the shortening, butter and egg in a mixing bowl and beat until smooth. Stir in the remaining cake mix. Roll the dough 1/4 inch thick on a floured surface. Cut as desired. Arrange on a baking pan. Bake at 375 degrees for 8 to 10 minutes. Poke holes in the baked cakes with a fork while still warm. Let stand until cool. Spread ice cream over half the cakes. Top with the remaining cakes. Freeze, covered, until firm.

Serves variable

Lemon Stacks

Juice of 1 lemon
1 (2-layer) package white cake mix
3 egg whites
Grated zest of 1 lemon
1/2 teaspoon lemon extract

2 teaspoons poppy seeds
1 1/2 cups whipped topping
1 (3-ounce) package lemon instant
  pudding mix
1/2 teaspoon lemon extract

Spray a 10x15-inch baking pan with cooking spray. Line the pan with waxed paper. Spray the waxed paper with cooking spray. Add enough water to the lemon juice to measure 1 1/3 cups. Combine the lemon juice mixture, cake mix, egg whites, lemon zest and 1/2 teaspoon lemon extract in a mixing bowl and beat for 3 minutes. Fold in the poppy seeds. Spread the mixture in the prepared pan.

Bake at 350 degrees for 20 minutes or until the cake springs back when lightly touched. Let cool in the pan on a wire rack for 10 minutes. Invert the cake onto the wire rack and let cool completely.

Combine the whipped topping, pudding mix and 1/2 teaspoon lemon extract in a mixing bowl and beat for 4 minutes or until thickened and smooth. Cut twenty-four 2 1/4-inch rounds from the cooled cake.

Arrange 12 cake rounds on a large platter. Spread 2 tablespoons of the filling over each cake round. Top with the remaining cake rounds and 1 rounded tablespoon of the filling. Serve immediately.

Serves 12

Strawberry Tarts

1 (2-layer) package yellow cake mix 2 cups strawberry jam
1 (2-crust) pie pastry

Prepare the cake mix using the package directions. Cut 24 rounds from the pie pastry. Fit into 24 greased muffin tins. Spoon 1 tablespoon jam over each pastry round. Pour the cake batter over the jam, filling the muffin tins 3/4 full. Bake at 350 degrees for 18 to 25 minutes or until the tart springs back when lightly touched. Cool in the muffin tins for 10 minutes. Remove to a wire rack to cool completely.

Serves 24

Apple Delight

2 (21-ounce) cans apple pie filling 1/2 cup (1 stick) butter, melted
1 (2-layer) package yellow cake mix

Pour the pie filling into a 9x13-inch baking pan. Sprinkle with the cake mix. Drizzle with the butter. Bake at 350 degrees for 30 minutes. Serve warm with vanilla ice cream.

Serves 18

Cherry Dump Dessert

1 (21-ounce) can cherry pie filling
1 (15-ounce) can crushed pineapple
1 (2-layer) package butter cake mix

2^1/$_2$ cups flaked coconut
1 cup halved pecans
1 cup (2 sticks) margarine, melted

Pour the pie filling into a 9x13-inch baking pan. Pour the undrained pineapple over the pie filling. Sprinkle with the cake mix and coconut. Sprinkle with the pecans. Drizzle with the margarine. Bake at 325 degrees for 40 minutes or until the top is golden brown.

Serves 18

Cranberry Cobbler

1 (21-ounce) can peach pie filling
1 (16-ounce) can whole cranberry
  sauce
1 (2-layer) package yellow cake mix
^{1}/$_2$ teaspoon cinnamon

^{1}/$_4$ teaspoon nutmeg
1 cup (2 sticks) butter or margarine,
  softened
^{1}/$_2$ cup chopped nuts

Combine the pie filling and cranberry sauce in a bowl and mix well. Spoon into a 9x13-inch baking pan. Combine the cake mix, cinnamon and nutmeg in a bowl and mix well. Cut in the butter with a pastry blender or 2 knives. Mix in the nuts. Sprinkle evenly over the fruit. Bake at 350 degrees for 45 to 50 minutes or until golden brown. Serve warm with whipped cream or ice cream.

Serves 10 to 12

Peach Cobbler

1 (29-ounce) can sliced peaches
1 (6-ounce) package peach gelatin
1 (2-layer) package yellow cake mix

$1/2$ cup (1 stick) butter, chopped
$1/2$ cup water

Drain the peaches, reserving the juice. Arrange the peaches in a 9x13-inch baking pan. Sprinkle the gelatin over the peaches. Sprinkle with the cake mix. Dot with the butter. Combine 1 cup of the reserved peach juice with the water. Pour over the layers. Bake at 350 degrees for 60 minutes or until the top is golden brown. Serve warm with whipped cream or ice cream.

Serves 10 to 12

Pumpkin Cobbler

1 (2-layer) package yellow cake mix
$1/2$ cup (1 stick) butter or margarine, softened
1 egg
1 (30-ounce) can pumpkin
3 eggs
$2/3$ cup evaporated milk

1 teaspoon vanilla extract
1 teaspoon cinnamon
1 cup packed brown sugar
$1/2$ cup sugar
$1/4$ cup ($1/2$ stick) butter or margarine, softened
Chopped pecans (optional)

Reserve 1 cup of the cake mix. Combine the remaining cake mix, $1/2$ cup butter and 1 egg in a bowl and mix well. Press into a 9x13-inch baking pan. Combine the pumpkin, 3 eggs, evaporated milk, vanilla, cinnamon and brown sugar in a bowl and mix well. Pour over the prepared layer. Combine the reserved cake mix, sugar and $1/4$ cup butter in a bowl and mix until crumbly. Sprinkle over the pumpkin mixture. Sprinkle with pecans. Bake at 350 degrees for 45 to 50 minutes or until brown. Serve warm with whipped topping.

Serves 10 to 12

Easy Strawberry Shortcake

1 (2-layer) package white
  cake mix
1 (12-ounce) can evaporated milk

2 (10-ounce) packages frozen
  strawberries, thawed and drained
12 ounces whipped topping

Prepare and bake the cake using the package directions for a 9x13-inch cake pan. Let cool slightly. Poke holes in the cake with a fork. Drizzle with the evaporated milk. Top with the strawberries. Spread the whipped topping over the strawberries. Chill, covered, until ready to serve.

Serves 12

Slow-Cooker Chocolate Cake

1 (4-ounce) package chocolate
  instant pudding mix
1 (2-layer) chocolate cake mix
2 cups sour cream

4 eggs
1 cup water
3/4 cup vegetable oil
1 cup chocolate chips

Combine the pudding mix, cake mix, sour cream, eggs, water and oil in a mixing bowl and beat for 2 minutes or until smooth. Stir in the chocolate chips. Spoon into a slow cooker. Cook on Low for 6 to 7 hours. Serve warm with whipped topping or ice cream.

Serves 16

Boston Cream Cheesecake

1 (9-ounce) package yellow cake mix
16 ounces cream cheese, softened
1/2 cup sugar
1 teaspoon vanilla extract
2 eggs
1/3 cup sour cream

2 tablespoons cold water
2 ounces unsweetened chocolate
3 tablespoons margarine
1 cup confectioners' sugar
1 teaspoon vanilla extract
Strawberries

Grease the bottom of a 9-inch springform pan. Prepare the cake mix using the package directions. Pour the batter into the prepared pan. Bake at 350 degrees for 20 minutes. Combine the cream cheese, sugar and 1 teaspoon vanilla in a mixing bowl and beat until blended. Add the eggs 1 at a time, beating well after each addition. Add the sour cream and mix well. Spread over the baked layer. Bake for 35 minutes longer. Cool in the pan for several minutes. Loosen the cake from the rim. Let cool completely. Remove the rim of the pan.

Bring the water to a boil in a saucepan. Add the chocolate and margarine. Cook until melted, stirring frequently. Combine the chocolate mixture and confectioners' sugar in a mixing bowl and beat well. Add 1 teaspoon vanilla and mix well. Spread over the cheesecake. Chill for several hours. Garnish with strawberries.

Yield: 10 to 12 servings

When preparing a cheesecake, make sure that all the ingredients are at room temperature so lumps don't form in the cream cheese.

Cherry Cheesecake

Chocolate Crust

1/4 cup (1/2 stick) butter, chopped
1 cup milk chocolate chips
1/3 cup water
1 (2-layer) package chocolate
   cake mix

1 egg
3/4 cup chopped pecans

Filling

1 (21-ounce) can cherry pie filling
24 ounces cream cheese, softened
3/4 cup sugar

3 eggs
1 teaspoon almond extract or vanilla
   extract

For the crust, combine the butter, chocolate chips and water in a saucepan over medium heat. Cook until the butter and chocolate chips are melted, stirring frequently. Remove from the heat and let cool slightly. Combine the cake mix and chocolate mixture in a large mixing bowl and beat until blended. Beat in the egg. Stir in the pecans. Spread the mixture over the bottom of a 9-inch springform pan sprayed with nonstick cooking spray.

For the filling, drain the cherries, reserving the sauce. Rinse the cherries and pat dry. Chop the cherries. Combine the cream cheese and sugar in a mixing bowl and beat until smooth. Add the eggs 1 at a time, beating well after each addition. Stir in the almond extract and cherries. Pour evenly over the crust.

Bake at 350 degrees for 50 to 55 minutes or until the center is almost set. Cool in the pan on a wire rack for 10 minutes. Spread 1 cup of the reserved cherry sauce over the top. Let stand until cool. Chill for 4 hours or longer.

Serves 16

Fruit Pizza

Crust
1 (2-layer) package yellow cake mix
$1/4$ cup water
$1/4$ cup packed light brown sugar

$1/4$ cup ($1/2$ stick) butter, melted
2 eggs

Topping
16 ounces whipped topping
2 cups sliced strawberries
1 (15-ounce) can pineapple chunks,
   drained

2 cups thinly sliced bananas
1 (11-ounce) can mandarin oranges,
   drained

Apricot Glaze
$1/2$ cup apricot preserves

2 tablespoons water

For the crust, lightly spray two 12- to 14-inch pizza pans with nonstick cooking spray. Line the pans with parchment paper or waxed paper. Lightly spray the paper with nonstick cooking spray. Dust with flour.

Combine the cake mix, water, brown sugar, butter and eggs in a large mixing bowl and beat at low speed for 1 to 2 minutes or until blended. The dough will be stiff and sticky. Spread the dough over the bottom and up the side of the prepared pans. Bake at 350 degrees for 18 to 22 minutes or until light brown and firm in the center. Let cool completely.

For the topping, spread the whipped topping over the crusts. Arrange the strawberries, pineapple, bananas and mandarin oranges over the whipped topping in concentric circles.

For the glaze, combine the apricot preserves and water in a small saucepan. Cook over low heat until warm, stirring constantly. Strain the mixture, discarding the apricot solids. Brush the apricot glaze over the fruit. Chill, uncovered, for 1 hour or longer.

Serves 16

Index